Excel Formulas and Functions

80 Top Excel Functions Made Easy

Nathan George

Excel Formulas and Functions: 80 Top Excel Functions Made Easy

Published 2022.

Published by GTech Publishing.

ISBN: 978-1-915476-08-1

Contents

Introduction

Excel Formulas and Functions covers the most useful functions in each category of Excel functions based on how often they're used in everyday Excel tasks and specialized work. Excel functions can save you a lot of time and effort as they're predefined formulas that only need you to provide the input values. Functions help to reduce errors in your formulas as they are tried and tested. Knowing what Excel tools are available to you enables you to be more creative with your spreadsheet solutions.

My *Excel 2022 Basics* book covered the most commonly used functions in everyday Excel tasks. This book goes beyond the basics and covers functions like IFS and other advanced functions for lookup and reference, text manipulation, statistics, and finance. You also learn to combine functions to create formulas for more complex problems.

This book covers each function in detail using appropriate practical examples and step-by-step explanations. The lessons are concise and straightforward, as the aim is to provide you with solutions for your data as quickly as possible without needing to wade through a ton of text.

Who This Book Is For

This book is for you if you want to learn more about Excel functions and if you need a functions companion guide when working with Excel. *Excel Formulas and*

Functions provides a treasure trove of ideas and solutions for better ways of approaching Excel problems.

This book assumes you have some basic knowledge of Excel. For brevity, foundational topics that have already been covered in my *Excel 2022 Basics* book have not been covered here again. If you need to brush up on the basics (or if you're new to Excel), my *Excel 2022 Basics* book covers all the foundation knowledge you'll need.

Some functions covered in this book are currently only available to Microsoft 365 subscribers. However, if you have a previous standalone version of Excel, like Excel 2019 or 2016, you'll still find many lessons in this book relevant, as most of the functions covered are available in previous versions of Excel.

How to Use This Book

This book has been designed as a reference manual or a companion guide you have at hand as you work with Excel. You can read the chapters in sequential order or pick and choose which topics you want to cover. As much as possible, each function in this book has been covered as a standalone tutorial. A side effect of this is that there will be some repetition, as it is not assumed that you're reading the chapters in sequential order.

Some examples use multi-function solutions, but all functions used in the included examples are covered individually in the book. The functions have also been organized into categories to make it easier to find the correct function for a specific problem you want to address.

Assumptions

The software assumptions made when writing this book are that you already have Excel installed on your computer and you're working on the Windows 11 (or Windows 10) platform. If you are using Excel on a Mac, substitute any Windows keyboard commands mentioned in the book for the Mac equivalent. All the features within Excel remain the same for both platforms.

If you're using Excel on a tablet or touchscreen device, simply substitute any keyboard commands mentioned in the book with the equivalent on your touchscreen device.

Practice Files

Downloadable Excel practice files have been provided to make it easier to learn Excel formulas and functions. All examples are fully detailed in the book, so the practice files are optional. You can practice by changing the data to view different results. You can also copy and use the predefined formulas in your own worksheets. You can download the files from the following link:

https://www.excelbytes.com/excel-formulas-dl

Notes:

- Type the URL in your Internet browser's address bar, and press Enter to navigate to the download page. If you encounter an error, double-check that you have correctly entered all characters in the URL.

- The files have been zipped into one download. Windows 10 and 11 come with the functionality to unzip files. If your OS does not have this functionality, you'll need to get a piece of software like WinZip or WinRAR to unzip the file.

- The files are Excel 365 files, so you will need to have Excel installed on your computer to open and use these files (preferably Excel 2013 and above).

- If you have any problems downloading these files, please contact me at **support@excelbytes.com**. Include the title of this book in your email, and the practice files will be emailed directly to you.

Chapter 1

Formula Basics

This chapter covers the following:

- How to enter a formula in Excel.

- Operators in Excel and how operator precedence affects your formula results.

- How to step through a formula and fix errors using Evaluate Formula.

How to Enter a Formula

To insert a formula in a cell, do the following:

1. Click the cell where you want to display the result.

2. Click in the formula bar.

3. Enter your formula, starting your entry with the equal sign (=). The equal sign tells Excel that your entry is a formula, not a static value.

4. Press **Enter** on your keyboard to confirm the entry. Alternatively, click the **Enter** button (check mark).

For example:

=SUM(A2:A10)

A11	⌄ ⋮ ✕ ✓ *fx*	=SUM(A2:A10)

	A	B	C	D	E
1					
2	12				
3	40				
4	68				
5	409				
6	217				
7	327				
8	85				
9	312				
10	369				
11	A10)				
12					

> **Tip** As much as possible, avoid typing cell references directly into the formula bar, as it could introduce errors. Instead, enter the name of the formula and then an open bracket. For example, enter =SUM(. Then select the cells you want for your argument in the worksheet itself before entering the closing bracket.

The Insert Function Dialog Box

A second way to enter a function is by using the **Insert Function** dialog box.

Click in the formula bar to place the cursor there. And then, click the **Insert Function** command on the **Formulas** tab or the Insert Function button next to the formula bar.

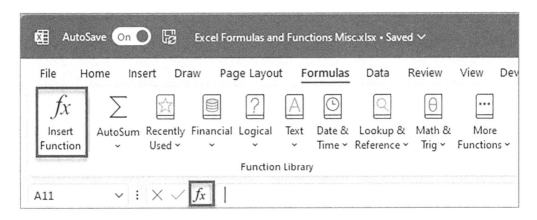

Excel displays the **Insert Function** dialog box. This dialog box provides the option to search for the function or select it from a category.

To search for the function, enter the function's name in the **Search for a function** box. For example, if you were searching for the IF function, you would enter IF in the search box and click **Go**. The **Select a function** list will display all the functions related to your search term.

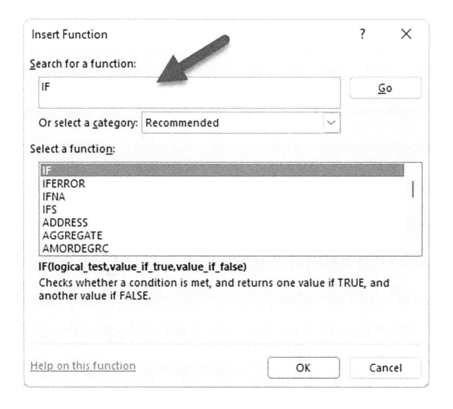

You can also use the **category** drop-down list to select a function if you know its category in Excel. For example, you can find the IF function in the **Logical** category.

If you have used a function recently, it'll be listed in the **Most Recently Used** category.

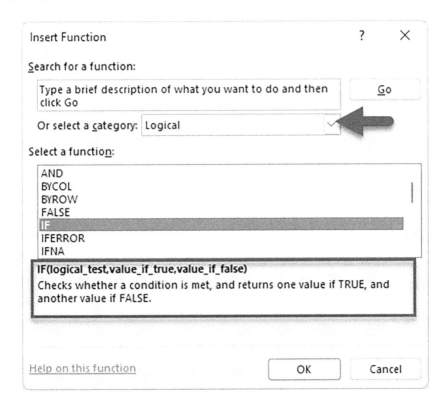

When you select a function on the list, you'll see the syntax and a description of what the function does below the list.

Once you've selected the function you want, click **OK** to open the Function Arguments dialog box.

The **Function Arguments** dialog box enables you to enter the arguments for the function. A function argument is a value the function needs to run.

The Function Arguments dialog box is particularly useful if you are unfamiliar with a function. It describes each argument, a preview of your entries, and the result returned by the function.

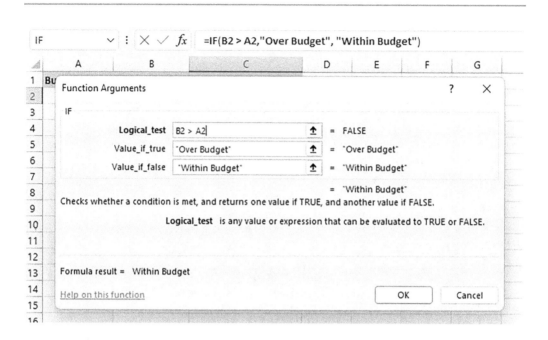

After entering the arguments, click **OK** to insert the formula in the formula bar.

Operators in Excel

Operators in Excel formulas specify the type of calculation to perform. For example, addition, subtraction, multiplication, or division. You can use four types of operators in Excel formulas: arithmetic, comparison, reference, and text.

This section covers these operators, examples of their use, and how operator precedence in Excel affects your results. We also cover how to change the order of operations with parentheses.

Arithmetic Operators

The following arithmetic operators are used to perform basic mathematical operations such as addition, subtraction, multiplication, and division.

Arithmetic operator	Meaning	Example
+ (plus sign)	Addition	=4+4
– (minus sign)	Subtraction	=4-4
		=-4
	Negation	
* (asterisk)	Multiplication	=4*4
/ (forward slash)	Division	=4/4
% (percent sign)	Percent	40%
^ (caret)	Exponentiation	=4^4

Comparison Operators

Comparison operators allow you to compare two values and produce a logical result, that is, TRUE or FALSE.

Comparison operator	Meaning	Example
=	Equal to	=A1=B1
>	Greater than	=A1>B1
<	Less than	=A1<B1
>=	Greater than or equal to	=A1>=B1
<=	Less than or equal to	=A1<=B1
<>	Not equal to	=A1<>B1

Reference Operators

Reference operators allow you to combine ranges of cells to create references for calculations.

Operator	Meaning	Example
: (colon)	Range operator. Creates one reference to the area between the cells.	A1:B10
(single space)	Intersection operator. References cells common to the two ranges.	=SUM(B7:D7 C6:C8)
,(comma)	Union operator. Combines several references into one.	=SUM(A1:A10,D1:D10)
#	Spilled range operator. Used to reference the range of a spilled result. The # symbol is also used as part of Excel error names like #REF!, and for indicating insufficient space for a value in a cell, for example, #####.	=AVERAGE(F3#)

Text Operator

The ampersand (&) is the only text operator in Excel. It enables you to join multiple text strings or cell values to produce a single text value.

Operator	Meaning	Example
&	Connects two strings of text (concatenation)	=A1 & " " & B1

Operator Precedence

If you combine several operators in a single formula, Excel performs the operations in the following order.

Operator	Description
: (colon)	Reference operators
(single space)	
,(comma)	
–	Negation (as in –4)
%	Percent
^	Exponentiation
* and /	Multiplication and division
+ and –	Addition and subtraction
&	Concatenation. Connects two text values or strings.
=	Comparison
<>	
<=	
>=	
<>	

At a basic level, you just need to remember that Excel performs multiplication and division before addition and subtraction. Excel will evaluate the operators from left to right if a formula contains operators with the same precedence, for instance, multiplication and division.

Parentheses and Operator Precedence

You can change the order of evaluation by enclosing parts of your formula in parentheses (). The part of the formula in parentheses will be calculated first.

For example, the following formula produces 75 because Excel calculates multiplication before addition. So, Excel multiplies 7 by 10 before adding 5 to the result.

=5+7*10

Answer = 75

In contrast, if we enclose 5+7 in parentheses, Excel will calculate 5 + 7 first before multiplying the result by 7 to produce 120.

=(5+7)*10

Answer = 120

In another example, we want to add 20% to 300. The parentheses around the second part of the formula ensure Excel calculates the addition before the multiplication to produce 360.

=300 * (1 + 0.2)

Answer = 360

How to Step Through a Formula

Occasionally you may encounter a formula that's not returning the expected result, but it is not generating one of the standard Excel errors. These types of errors are called logical errors and can be the hardest to diagnose if you have a complex formula with several nested levels.

In a complex formula with several levels of logical tests, it may be challenging to keep track of the sequence of operations and what results are being returned at each level. To help with troubleshooting formulas, Excel provides a tool called **Evaluate Formula** that allows you to step through a formula. Evaluate Formula enables you to examine the items evaluated, the sequence, and the results. Hence, this tool enables you to identify and fix any logical errors in your syntax.

In the following example, we'll use Evaluate Formula to evaluate the following nested formula:

=IF(D2 >= 10000,IF(E2 >= 15,D2*0.2,D2*0.15),IF(E2 >= 15,D2*0.15,D2*0.1))

The formula calculates the following:

- If a sales rep generates $10,000 in sales AND 15 signups, they earn a 20% commission on their sales amount.

- If a sales rep generates either $10,000 in sales OR 15 signups, they earn a 15% commission on their sales amount.

- If a sales rep generates less than $10,000 in sales and less than 15 signups, they earn a 10% commission on their sales amount.

The data being evaluated is shown in the image below.

fx	=IF(D2 >= 10000,IF(E2 >= 15,D2*0.2,D2*0.15),IF(E2 >= 15,D2*0.15,D2*0.1))

C	D	E	F	G	H
Sales rep	Sales	Signups	Commission		
Gilbert Higgins	$12,500	20	$2,500		
Clinton Bradley	$14,300	25	$2,860		
Bob Nash	$9,000	10	$900		
Lee Powers	$8,050	5	$805		
Mae Stevens	$5,000	7	$500		
Inez Griffith	$8,900	10	$890		
Theresa Hawkins	$7,900	10	$790		
Felix Jacobs	$6,000	17	$900		
Erik Lane	$11,000	18	$2,200		
Jesse Garza	$12,676	12	$1,901		
Alberta Fletcher	$13,163	14	$1,975		
Melody Mendoza	$8,795	20	$1,319		
Abraham Graves	$12,875	26	$2,575		
Van Sims	$6,646	16	$997		

Follow the steps below to evaluate a formula:

1. Select the cell that you want to evaluate. In our example, it would be cell **F2**. Note that Excel can only evaluate one cell at a time.

2. On the **Formulas** tab, in the **Formula Auditing** group, click on the **Evaluate Formula** button.

   Excel opens the **Evaluate Formula** dialog box. In the **Evaluation** box, Excel displays the formula being evaluated and underlines the next statement to be evaluated.

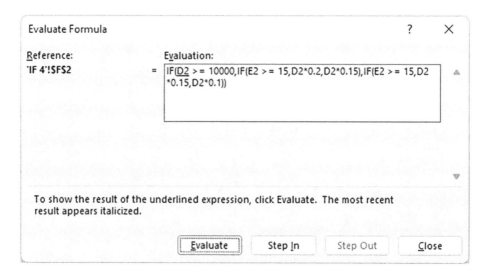

3. Click **Evaluate**. Excel evaluates the underlined statement and shows the result in italics. The next item to be evaluated is then underlined.

    =IF(*12500* >= 1000,IF(E2 >= 15,D2*0.2,D2*0.15),IF(E2 >= 15,D2*0.15,D2*0.1))

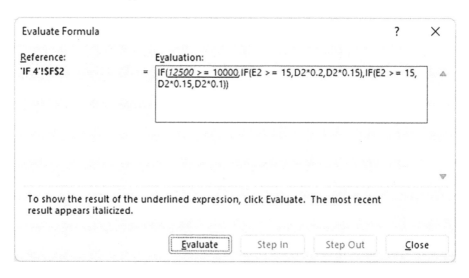

4. Click **Evaluate** again to evaluate the underlined statement. Excel shows the result in italics and underlines the next item to be evaluated.

    =IF(*TRUE*,IF(E2 >= 15,D2*0.2,D2*0.15),IF(E2 >= 15,D2*0.15,D2*0.1))

    In this case, the result of the test is TRUE. Hence, Excel will process elements of the first nested IF statement.

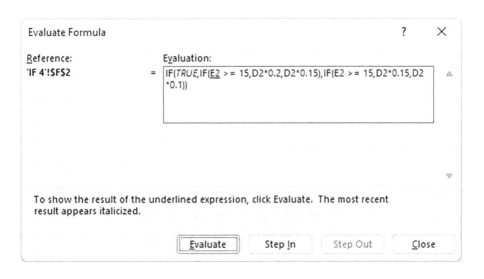

5. Click **Evaluate** to step through the formula and view the results until the final value is displayed in the **Evaluation** box.

   If there is a logical error in your formula, you should be able to identify it here by stepping through the formula. Pay attention to each element being evaluated and the result returned.

6. Click **Restart** if you want to step through the formula again.

7. Click **Close** to dismiss the Evaluate Formula dialog box.

Chapter 2

Lookup and Reference Functions

In this chapter, we'll cover functions that enable you to:

- Lookup data in a list, table, or range based on one or more lookup values.

- Perform complex vertical and horizontal lookups.

- Transpose a column or row of data using.

- Choose a value from a list, table, or range based on a search index.

- Return the address of a cell in your worksheet.

- Display the formula of a cell (rather than the return value).

- Return the number of rows or columns in a range.

- Select and return a subset of rows or columns.

The Lookup and Reference functions can be found by clicking the **Lookup & Reference** command button on the **Formulas** tab on the Ribbon. Excel provides many functions to enable you to look up one piece of data using another. Reference functions allow you to find and return specific information about your data.

Looking Up Values in a Range

The functions in this section enable you to look up one value based on another. You can perform complex lookups using more than one value to search for and return a value or an array.

Find Data with XLOOKUP

XLOOKUP was introduced as an improvement on the VLOOKUP function. Like its predecessor, XLOOKUP searches a range or an array and returns a value corresponding to the first match it finds on the same row in another range.

For instance, you can look up the **price** of a product in a data list using the **Product ID** or **name**. Similarly, you can return an employee's name using their employee ID. If XLOOKUP does not find a match, you can tell it to return the closest (approximate) match.

Unlike VLOOKUP, which only allows you to return values from a column to the right of the lookup range, XLOOKUP can return values from columns to the left or the right of the lookup range. XLOOKUP also returns exact matches by default, making it easier and more convenient than its predecessor.

> **Note** The XLOOKUP function is available in Excel for Microsoft 365 and Excel 2021. If you're using an older 'standalone version' of Excel, XLOOKUP will not be available.

Syntax:

=XLOOKUP(lookup_value, lookup_array, return_array, [if_not_found], [match_mode], [search_mode])

Arguments and Descriptions

Argument	Description
lookup_value	Required. What value are you searching for? Excel will look for a match for this value in the lookup_array. You can provide a value here or a cell reference containing the value you want to find.
lookup_array	Required. Where do you want to search? This value is the lookup range containing the columns you want to include in your search, for example, A2:D10.
return_array	Required. Which range contains the values you want to return? This value is the return range. The return range can have one or more columns, as XLOOKUP is about to return more than one value.
[if_not_found]	Optional. This optional argument enables you to enter a piece of text to return if a valid match is not found.
	If this argument is omitted and a valid match is not found, XLOOKUP will return the #N/A error.
[match_mode]	Optional. This optional argument enables you to specify a match mode from four options:
	0 (or omitted) = Exact match. If no match is found, Excel returns an error (#N/A), the default if you omit this argument.
	-1 = Exact match or the next smallest item if an exact match is not found.
	1 = Exact match or the next largest item if an exact match is not found.
	2 = Performs a wildcard match where you can use the characters *, ?, and ~ for wildcard searches.

[search_mode]   Optional. This optional argument enables you to specify the order in which you want to perform the search:

1 (or omitted) = Search first to last. This setting is the default if this argument is omitted.

-1 = Perform the search in reverse order - last to first.

2 = Perform a binary search for data sorted in ascending order. If lookup_array is not sorted in ascending order, invalid results will be returned.

-2 = Perform a binary search for data sorted in descending order. If lookup_array is not sorted in descending order, invalid results will be returned.

> **Tip**
> Regarding the *search_mode* argument, in earlier versions of Excel, performing binary searches on sorted lists produced quicker results, but in Microsoft 365, non-binary searches are equally fast. Hence, using binary search options for sorted lists is no longer beneficial. Using 1 or -1 for the search_mode argument is easier because you don't require a sorted table.

Vertical Lookup

In this example, we use XLOOKUP to return the Reorder Level of the product entered in cell F1. The formula is in cell F2.

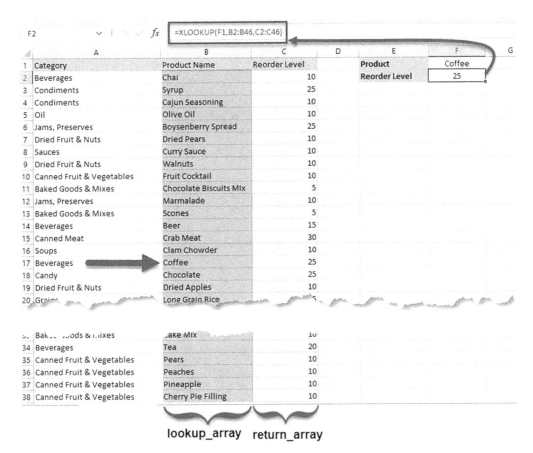

lookup_array   return_array

Formula explanation:

=XLOOKUP(F1,B2:B46,C2:C46)

The formula says, in range B2:B46, find the value in cell F1 (which in this case is "Coffee") and return the value on the same row in range C2:C46.

The *if_not_found* argument has not been provided here, so if a match is not found, it will return an error which is the default behavior.

The VLOOKUP equivalent of this formula would look like this:

=VLOOKUP(F1,B2:C46,2,0)

One benefit of using the XLOOKUP equivalent over this formula is that if we decide to insert a column between columns B and C at some point, it will not break the formula.

The lookup_array does not need to be sorted because XLOOKUP will return an exact match by default.

Horizontal Lookup

XLOOKUP can perform both vertical and horizontal lookups. Therefore, you can use it in place of the HLOOKUP function.

In the example below, we can retrieve the value associated with a month using the abbreviation of the month.

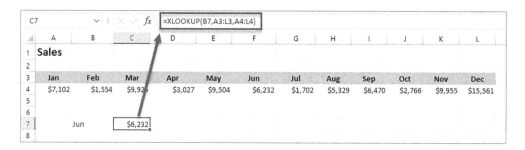

=XLOOKUP(B7,A3:L3,A4:L4)

The formula uses only the first three arguments of the XLOOKUP function. B7 is the lookup_value, A3:L3 is the lookup_array, and A4:L4 is the return_array.

Note that a horizontal lookup_array must contain the same number of columns as the return_array.

Simultaneous Vertical and Horizontal Lookup

This example will use two XLOOKUP functions to perform both a vertical and horizontal match. Here, the formula will first look for a "Mark" in the cell range A4:A15, then look for "Q3" in the top row of the table (range B3:E3) and return the value at the intersection of the two. Previously, you would need to use the INDEX/MATCH/MATCH combination to achieve the same result.

I4				f_x	=XLOOKUP(G4,A4:A15,XLOOKUP(H4,B3:E3,B4:E15))					
	A	B	C	D	E	F	G	H	I	J
1	**Sales data**									
2										
3	Salesperson	Q1	Q2	Q3	Q4					
4	Penny	17,526	23,972	61,066	22,596		Mark	Q3	19,062	
5	Leslie	49,405	36,646	21,899	62,629					
6	Sally	78,658	16,529	14,976	68,184					
7	Shaun	80,176	84,918	66,561	65,326					
8	Julie	86,988	29,692	30,197	80,960					
9	Velma	94,514	13,333	78,000	59,718					
10	Ian	23,183	21,547	40,408	57,767					
11	Cassandra	70,597	19,615	54,664	68,175					
12	Mark	16,832	91,907	19,062	33,167					
13	Kathy	45,446	14,638	52,312	92,069					
14	Renee	34,583	78,213	21,295	26,964					
15	Judith	18,689	91,081	66,795	96,860					

Formula explanation:

=XLOOKUP(G4,A4:A15,XLOOKUP(H4,B3:E3,B4:E15))

The first XLOOKUP function has the following arguments:

- lookup_value = G4
- lookup_array = A4:A15
- return_array = XLOOKUP(H4,B3:E3,B4:E15)

The second XLOOKUP, executed first, performs a horizontal search on B3:E3, using the value in cell H4 ("Q3") as the lookup_value, then returns the range **D4:D15**. Notice that the second XLOOKUP returns a range rather than a value. This range is used as the return_array argument for the first XLOOKUP.

So, after the second XLOOKUP has been executed, the first XLOOKUP will look like this:

=XLOOKUP(G4,A4:A15,D4:D15)

Examining the Formula with Evaluate Formula

To examine how the formula performs the task, you can use the **Evaluate Formula** dialog box in Excel to see how each formula part is evaluated.

Follow the steps below to open the Evaluate Formula dialog box:

1. Select the cell with the formula you want to evaluate. In this case, it is cell **I4**.

2. On the Formulas tab, in the **Formula Auditing** group, click the **Evaluate Formula** command button.

3. In the Evaluate Formula dialog box, click the **Evaluate** button until the nested XLOOKUP function has been evaluated and its result is displayed in the formula.

   For this example, we need to click the Evaluate button three times.

You will notice that the second XLOOKUP performs a search using the lookup_value, "Q3", and then returns the range **D4:D15** (displayed as an absolute reference $**D$4:$D$15**). We can use XLOOKUP here as the *return_array* argument of the first XLOOKUP function because XLOOKUP can return a range and value.

Next, the main XLOOKUP performs a lookup using the value in cell G4, "Mark" as the lookup_value, cells A4:A15 as the lookup_array, and cells D4:D15 as the return_array to return the final result.

Return Multiple Values with Horizontal Spill

In this example, we want to be able to enter the name of a sales rep and return the number of orders and sales associated with them. Hence, the function will return more than one value. XLOOKUP is also an array function because it can return an array of values from the return_array.

In the formula below, the lookup_value is in cell G2, the *lookup_array* argument is A2:A12, and the *return_array* argument is the cell range C2:D12.

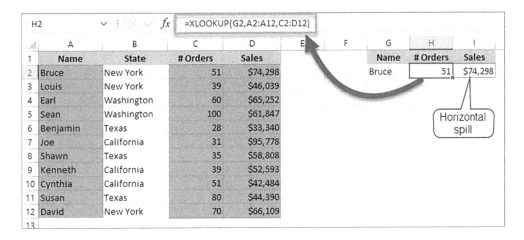

Formula explanation:

=XLOOKUP(G2,A2:A12,C2:D12)

As you can see from the formula, the return_array contains columns C and D. When we enter the name "Bruce" in cell G2, XLOOKUP returns the values in columns C and D from the same row. As the function returns more than one value, the result spills into cell I2.

The range containing the spilled result has a blue border, which is how you can tell the result has spilled into other cells.

Return Multiple Values with Vertical Spill

To get the formula to spill vertically, we can use another example where we need to return the sales for more than one person on our list.

In this example, we first use the FILTER function to generate a filtered list of names based in **New York**. The function returns an array of names that spill vertically in the range G2:G4.

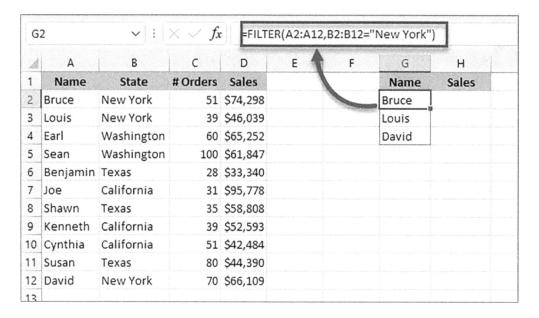

Next, we want to get the **Sales** associated with the names on our filtered list and insert them in column H. To do this, we use XLOOKUP in cell H2 and select cells G2:G4 for our lookup_value argument.

When you select the *lookup_value* (G2:G4), Excel recognizes the range as a spilled range and references the range with the spilled range operator, i.e., G2#.

	A	B	C	D	E	F	G	H
H2			fx	=XLOOKUP(G2#,A2:A12,D2:D12)				
1	Name	State	# Orders	Sales			Name	Sales
2	Bruce	New York	51	$74,298			Bruce	$74,298
3	Louis	New York	39	$46,039			Louis	$46,039
4	Earl	Washington	60	$65,252			David	$66,109
5	Sean	Washington	100	$61,847				
6	Benjamin	Texas	28	$33,340				
7	Joe	California	31	$95,778				
8	Shawn	Texas	35	$58,808				
9	Kenneth	California	39	$52,593				
10	Cynthia	California	51	$42,484				
11	Susan	Texas	80	$44,390				
12	David	New York	70	$66,109				
13								
14								
15								

Formula explanation:

=XLOOKUP(G2#,A2:A12,D2:D12)

The lookup_value argument in the formula is G2#.

G2# (note the hash) designates the entire range of the spilled data. It tells us that G2 is the starting point of the array of values returned from a dynamic array formula.

The lookup_array is the Name column (A2:A12), and the return_array is the Sales column (D2:D12).

When you type in the formula in cell H2 and press Enter, XLOOKUP will return all the sales related to the names in the dynamic array in column G. As we have more than one value, it will spill down vertically in column H2.

One benefit of using XLOOKUP is that the formula will adjust to the dynamic array in column G. If we change the filter and add more names to column G, the formula in cell H2 would still work in finding the values corresponding to the new names. We don't have to worry about copying the formula to additional cells.

Common XLOOKUP Errors and Solutions

#N/A error

If an exact match is not found, and the **if_not_found** and **match_mode** arguments are omitted, XLOOKUP will return a #N/A error.

There may be scenarios where you will not know if your formula will generate this error, for example, when a formula is copied to multiple cells in a column. If you want to catch and replace this error with a meaningful message, specify the message in the **if_not_found** argument.

For example:
=XLOOKUP(F2,B2:B12,D2:D12,"Item not found")

#VALUE! error

This error is often generated because the lookup and return arrays are not the same length. When you get this error, check that these ranges are the same length. The lookup_array and return_array should have the same number of rows for vertical lookups. If the lookup is horizontal, they should have the same number of columns.

#NAME? in cell

This error usually means that there is an issue with a cell reference. A typo in the cell reference or omitting the colon can generate this error. When you get this error, check your cell references. To help avoid errors and typos in your formula, select cell references on the worksheet with your mouse rather than typing them in the formula.

#REF! error

If XLOOKUP is referencing another workbook that is closed, you will get a #REF! error. Ensure all workbooks referenced in your formula are open to avoid this error.

#SPILL! error

When returning multiple values, if there is already data in the spill range, Excel returns the #SPILL! error. To avoid this error, ensure there is no existing data in the cells that will contain the returned results.

Find Data with VLOOKUP

VLOOKUP is still one of the most popular lookup functions in Excel despite the introduction of XLOOKUP. If you intend to share your workbook with people using older versions of Excel without XLOOKUP, you might want to use VLOOKUP for looking up data. VLOOKUP enables you to find one piece of information in a workbook based on another piece of information. For example, if you have a product list, you can find and return a **Product Code** by providing the corresponding **Product Name** to the VLOOKUP function.

Syntax

=VLOOKUP (lookup_value, table_array, col_index_num, [range_lookup])

Arguments

Argument	Description
lookup_value	Required. What value are you searching for? This argument is the lookup value. Excel will look for a match for this value in the leftmost column of your chosen range. You can provide a value here or a cell reference.
table_array	Required. What columns do you want to search? This argument is the range you want to include in your search, e.g., A2:D10.
col_index_num	Required. Which column contains the search result? Count from the first column to determine what this number should be, starting from 1.
range_lookup	Optional.
	For an exact match, enter FALSE/0.
	For an approximate match, enter TRUE/1.
	For TRUE, ensure the leftmost column is sorted in ascending order for correct results.
	This argument defaults to TRUE if omitted.

Example 1 – Standard lookup

In the example below, we use VLOOKUP to find the **Price** and **Reorder Level** of a product by entering the **Product Name** in cell G2. The formula is in cell G3, and as you can see from the image below, it searches the table for **Pears** and returns the price from the next column.

Formula Explanation

The following formula looks up the **Price** for **Pears**:

=VLOOKUP(G2, B2:D46, 2, FALSE)

The function uses a lookup_value from cell **G2** to search a table_array which is **B2:D46**.

The col_index_num is **2,** so it returns a value from the second column in the search range (table_array), the **Price** column.

The range_lookup is **FALSE**, meaning we want an exact match.

To look up the **Reorder Level** for Pears, we use the same formula and just change the column containing the search result (col_index_num) to 3 to return a value from the third row of the table array.

=VLOOKUP(G2, B2:D46, **3**, FALSE)

In this case, the VLOOKUP search for Pears returns a Reorder Level of **10**.

Example 2 - Approximate match

In the following example, we want to find an approximate match if an exact match is not found. The worksheet calculates the commission for each Sales Rep based on their sales. We have a Commission table to the right of the Sales report with a graduated scale of rates against sales.

We want to ensure that if an exact match is not found on the commission table, an approximate match is applied for the sales rep. $5,000 or more in sales is 2% commission, $10,000 or more is 5%, $20,000 or more is 10%, and so on.

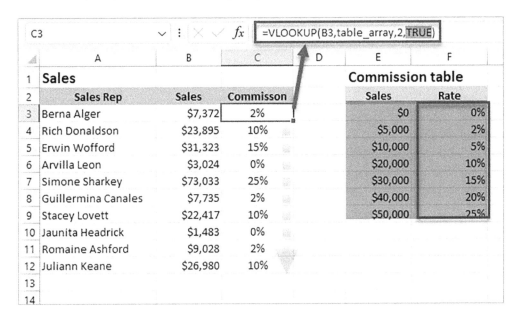

C3			f_x	=VLOOKUP(B3,table_array,2,TRUE)	

	A	B	C	D	E	F
1	Sales				Commission table	
2	Sales Rep	Sales	Commisson		Sales	Rate
3	Berna Alger	$7,372	2%		$0	0%
4	Rich Donaldson	$23,895	10%		$5,000	2%
5	Erwin Wofford	$31,323	15%		$10,000	5%
6	Arvilla Leon	$3,024	0%		$20,000	10%
7	Simone Sharkey	$73,033	25%		$30,000	15%
8	Guillermina Canales	$7,735	2%		$40,000	20%
9	Stacey Lovett	$22,417	10%		$50,000	25%
10	Jaunita Headrick	$1,483	0%			
11	Romaine Ashford	$9,028	2%			
12	Juliann Keane	$26,980	10%			
13						
14						

Formula Explanation:

=VLOOKUP(B3,table_array,2,TRUE)

The *lookup_value* is cell B3, the value for which we want an approximate match in the lookup range (cells E3:F9).

Note that the lookup range (E3:F9) is a named range, **table_array**. Named ranges are absolute references, ensuring cell references do not change when the formula is filled down to other cells.

The *col_index_num* is set to 2, meaning we want to return values from the second column in table_array.

The optional *range_lookup* argument is set to TRUE, which tells Excel to return an approximate match if an exact match is not found. The default for the *range_lookup* argument is TRUE if omitted, so you do not need to set this argument explicitly to TRUE. This example specifies it for demonstration purposes only.

Best Practices for VLOOKUP

- **Use absolute references for the table array.**

  Using absolute references allows you to fill down a formula without changing the cell references. An absolute reference ensures that VLOOKUP always looks at the same table array when the formula is copied to other cells.

- **Do not store a number or date as a text value.**

  When searching for numbers or dates, ensure the data in the first column of the table array is not stored as text. Otherwise, the formula might return an incorrect or unexpected value. Number and date values are right-aligned, while text values are left-aligned by default. Therefore, if your numbers or dates are left-aligned in the cell, you must check that they are using the right cell format.

- **Sort the first column.**

  If you want VLOOKUP to find the next best match when the **range_lookup** argument is TRUE, make sure the first column in **table_array** is sorted.

- **Use wildcard characters.**

  You can use a wildcard in **lookup_value** if **range_lookup** is FALSE and lookup_value is text. A question mark (?) matches any single character, and an asterisk (*) matches any sequence of characters. If you want to find an actual question mark or asterisk as part of the search criteria, type a tilde (~) in front of the character.

  For example, =VLOOKUP("Dried*",B2:D46,2,FALSE) will find the first item starting with "Dried" in the first column of table_array.

- **Make sure your data does not contain erroneous characters.**

  If you are searching for text values in the first column of the table array, ensure the data in the first column does not have leading or trailing spaces, non-printable characters, and inconsistent use of straight and curly quotation marks. In cases like these, the formula might return an unexpected value.

To clean up your data, you can use the TRIM function to remove any extra spaces or the CLEAN function to remove all nonprintable characters.

Common VLOOKUP Errors and Solutions

- **Wrong value returned**

  If you omit the **range_lookup** argument or set it to TRUE (for an approximate match), you need to sort the first column of **table_array** in alphanumeric order. Excel may return an unexpected value if the first column is not sorted. Use FALSE for an exact match or sort the first column of the table array for an approximate match.

- **#N/A error in cell**

  If the range_lookup argument is FALSE, and an exact match is not found, you will get a #N/A error. You will also get a #N/A error if **range_lookup** is TRUE and the **lookup_value** is smaller than the smallest value in the first column of **table_array**.

- **#REF! error in cell**

  You will get the #REF error if the col_index_num argument exceeds the number of columns in the table array.

- **#VALUE! error in cell**

  You will encounter a #VALUE! error if the **lookup_value** argument is over 255 characters. Use wildcards for partial matches if the values in the lookup range are over 255 characters.

  Excel will also generate the #VALUE! error if the **col_index_num** argument contains text or is less than 1. Ensure **col_index_num** is not less than 1.

- **#NAME? error in cell**

  This error usually means that the formula is missing quotes. If you enter a text value directly in your formula (instead of a cell reference), ensure you enclose the value in quotes. For example, =VLOOKUP("Dried Pears", B2:D46, 2, FALSE). You will also get this error if you make a mistake when typing in the cell reference. Select cell references on the worksheet with your mouse rather than typing them in the formula to avoid cell reference typos.

Find Data with HLOOKUP

HLOOKUP is now a legacy function in Excel, as you can perform horizontal lookups with XLOOKUP (see the section on XLOOKUP). However, if you have an older version of Excel without XLOOKUP, then you may need to use this function for horizontal lookups.

> **Tip** You can now use the new XLOOKUP function for horizontal lookups. It is an improvement on HLOOKUP. XLOOKUP does everything HLOOKUP can do and more. It is also easier and more convenient to use.

HLOOKUP searches for a value in the top row of a range or table and returns a value in the same column from a row you specify in the range or table. The function performs a horizontal search on the first column of the specified range for the lookup value (criteria). Then it uses the criteria to return another value from the same column but on a row below.

Use HLOOKUP when your lookup values are in a row at the top of a range or table, and you want to look down a specified number of rows. Conversely, VLOOKUP is suitable when your lookup values are in a column to the left of the data you want to search for.

Syntax

=HLOOKUP(lookup_value, table_array, row_index_num, [range_lookup])

Arguments

Argument	Description
lookup_value	Required. The search criteria. The value should be in the first row of table_array. Lookup_value can be text, a value, or a reference.
table_array	Required. A range or table which contains the data being looked up. You can use cell references or a named range.
row_index_num	Required. The row number from which you want the value returned, counting from 1 from the first row of the range.
range_lookup	Optional. This argument is to specify whether HLOOKUP should find an exact match or an approximate match. TRUE is for an approximate match, while FALSE is for an exact match. If this argument is omitted, it'll default to TRUE.

Example

E2				f_x	=HLOOKUP("Bolts",myList,6,FALSE)

◢	A	B	C	D	E	F
1	Spanners	Bolts	Wrenches		Result	Formula text
2	7	4	11		5	=HLOOKUP("Bolts",myList,6,FALSE)
3	6	7	10		6	=HLOOKUP("Spanners",myList,3,FALSE)
4	1	5	8		10	=HLOOKUP("Wrenches",myList,3,TRUE)
5	2	3	12		6	=HLOOKUP("Spanners",myList,3,FALSE)
6	9	5	8			
7						

Note that the range **A1:C6** has been named as **myList**. This type of name is known as a *named range* in Excel.

Formula explanations:

=HLOOKUP("Bolts",myList,6,FALSE)

This formula uses "Bolts" as the lookup value to return a value on row 6 from the same column.

=HLOOKUP("Spanners",myList,3,FALSE)

This formula uses "Spanners" as the lookup value to return a value on row 3 from the same column.

=HLOOKUP("Wrenches",myList,3,TRUE)

This formula uses "Wrenches" as the lookup value to return a value on row 3 from the same column.

MATCH Function

The MATCH function searches for a given item in a list and then returns the relative position of the item in the list. MATCH tells you where in your list you can locate your value after you provide search parameters. For example, if the range A1:A5 has the values 10, 30, 26, 44, and 100, the formula =MATCH(44,A1:A5,0) will return 4 because 44 is the fourth item in the range. If MATCH cannot find an exact match, it will find the closest item to the lookup criteria, which can be useful when you want to identify the cut-off point in a list of values.

MATCH is most useful when used as an argument inside another function where you need to return the position of a specific item on your list as one of the arguments for that function. MATCH is often used with the INDEX function to find and return items in a table.

> **Tip** If you're using Microsoft 365, try using the new XMATCH function. XMATCH is an improved version of MATCH that is easier and more convenient to use than its predecessor.

Syntax

=MATCH(lookup_value, lookup_array, [match_type])

Arguments

Argument	Description
lookup_value	Required. The value you want to match in your list. This argument can be a number, cell reference, text, or logical value.
lookup_array	Required. The list or range to be searched.
match_type	Optional. This argument specifies how the function will behave.
	You have three options for this argument -1, 0, or 1. The default is 1 if the argument is omitted.
	1 (or omitted) = MATCH finds the largest value that is less than or equal to the lookup value. The values in the list must be in ascending order.
	0 = MATCH finds the first value that's exactly equal to lookup_value. The values in the range can be in any order.
	-1 = MATCH finds the smallest value greater than or equal to lookup_value. The values in the list must be in descending order.

Remarks

- MATCH is not case-sensitive.

- If MATCH cannot find a matching, it returns a #N/A error.

- If the lookup_value is a text string and match_type is 0, you can use the wildcard characters, question mark (?), and asterisk (*) in the lookup_value argument. A question mark (?) matches any single character, while an asterisk (*) is used to match a sequence of characters. To find a question mark or asterisk as part of the criteria in lookup_value, type a tilde (~) before the character.

Example

In this example, MATCH is used to query the range A2:A10, named Products, to find the position of the lookup values entered in column C.

	A	B	C	D	E	F
	D2		⌄ ⋮ ✕ ✓ *fx*	=MATCH(C2,Products,0)		
	Product Name		**Lookup value**	**Matched row**	**Formula text**	
1						
2	Curry Sauce		Curry Sauce	1	=MATCH(C2,Products,0)	
3	Dried Pears		*Oil	4	=MATCH(C3,Products,0)	
4	Boysenberry Spread		Syrup	6	=MATCH(C4,Products,0)	
5	Olive Oil		Cajun*	5	=MATCH(C5,Products,0)	
6	Cajun Seasoning		Cha?	8	=MATCH(C6,Products,0)	
7	Syrup					
8	Walnuts					
9	Chai				*Products = A2:A10*	
10	Tomato Sauce					
11						
12						

Formula explanation

=MATCH(C2,Products,0)

In the above formula, the lookup_value is in cell C2, the lookup_array is the range Products, and the match_type is 0, indicating that we want an exact match.

Notice that some of the lookup values in column C have wildcard characters. When the match_type is 0, you can provide only part of the lookup_value with a question mark (?) or asterisk (*) to perform a wildcard search.

XMATCH Function

The XMATCH function is an improved version of the MATCH function. The MATCH function searches for a given item in a list and then returns the relative position of the item in the list. MATCH tells you where you can locate the value you've provided as the criteria in your list.

For example, if the range A1:A5 has the values 10, 30, 26, 44, and 100, the formula =MATCH(44,A1:A5,0) will return 4 because 44 is the fourth item in the range.

XMATCH is multidirectional and returns exact matches by default, which makes it easier to use than its predecessor.

XMATCH is often used in combination with another function. For example, you may want to find the position of a value in a list to use as an argument in another function. XMATCH is often used with the INDEX function for performing lookups.

Syntax

=XMATCH(lookup_value, lookup_array, [match_mode], [search_mode])

Argument	Description
lookup_value	Required. The value you want to match in your list. This argument can be a number, cell reference, text, or logical value.
lookup_array	Required. The list or range to be searched.
[match_mode]	Optional. This argument enables you to specify a match mode from four options: **0 (or omitted)** = Exact match. An error will be returned if no match is found (#N/A). This option is the default if you omit this argument. **-1** = Exact match or the next smallest item if an exact match is not found. **1** = Exact match or the next largest item if an exact match is not found.

	2 = Performs a wildcard match where you use *, ?, and ~.
[search_mode]	Optional. This argument enables you to specify the search mode to use:

1 (or omitted) = Search first to last. This option is the default if this argument is omitted.

-1 = Perform the search in reverse order - last to first.

2 = Perform a binary search (for data sorted in ascending order). If lookup_array is not sorted in ascending order, invalid results will be returned.

-2 = Perform a binary search (for data sorted in descending order). If lookup_array is not sorted in descending order, invalid results will be returned.

Examples

In the example below, we use XMATCH to find the relative position of products on the list based on different search criteria. The formulas also use different optional arguments to determine the function's behavior.

D2				f_x	=XMATCH(C2,$A$2:$A$12)

	A	B	C	D	E
1	Product		Product	Position	Formula Text
2	Chai		Walnuts	7	=XMATCH(C2,$A$2:$A$12)
3	Syrup		Wal?	7	=XMATCH(C3,$A$2:$A$12,1)
4	Cajun Seasoning		*Oil	4	=XMATCH(C4,$A$2:$A$12,2)
5	Olive Oil		*Sauce	6	=XMATCH(C5,$A$2:$A$12,2)
6	Dried Pears		*Sauce	11	=XMATCH(C6,$A$2:$A$12,2,-1)
7	Curry Sauce				
8	Walnuts				
9	Fruit Cocktail				
10	Chocolate Biscuits Mix				
11	Marmalade				
12	Tomato Sauce				

Formula explanation:

=XMATCH(C2,$A$2:$A$12)

This example is a straightforward search for "Walnuts" (cell C2), and the formula returns its relative position of 7 on the list. The optional arguments have been omitted here, so the function uses its default search behavior.

=XMATCH(C3,$A$2:$A$12,1)

In this example, the *match_mode* argument has been set to 1, which tells XMATCH to find the position of the first item that is an exact match or the next largest value that starts with "Wal."

=XMATCH(C4,$A$2:$A$12,2)

In this example, the *match_mode* argument has been set to 2, which specifies that we are performing a wildcard search. Thus, the wildcard characters (*, ?, and ~) are treated as special characters.

=XMATCH(C6,$A$2:$A$12,2,-1)

In this example, the *match_mode* argument has been set to **2** for a wildcard search. The *search_mode* argument is set to **-1**, telling XMATCH to start from the last item.

You can see that the same search term, "*Sauce" in cells C5 and C6 returned different relative positions (6 and 11) because the formula in D5 is searching from the top. As a result, it finds "Curry Sauce" first. Conversely, the formula in D6 starts searching from the bottom, so it finds "Tomato Sauce" first.

INDEX Function

The INDEX function enables you to return a value or a series of values from a given location in range. The INDEX function is often combined with XMATCH (or its predecessor, MATCH) to perform horizontal and vertical lookups.

There are two forms of the INDEX function:
- Array form
- Reference form

Both INDEX forms are similar in behavior, but the Reference form enables you to specify multiple arrays, including an optional argument to select which array to use.

INDEX Function - Array Form

The array form of this function can return a single value or multiple values. If your formula returns more than one value, the results are spilled into adjacent cells to the right of the cell with the formula.

Syntax

=INDEX(array, row_num, [column_num])

Arguments

Argument	Description
array	Required. The array argument is a range of cells or an array constant. If the range contains only one row or column, the corresponding row_num or column_num is optional.
row_num	Required if column_num is omitted. This value specifies the row in the array argument from which to return a value.
column_num	Optional. Specifies the column in the array argument from which to return a value. If omitted, row_num is required.

Remarks

- If the *array* has more than one row and more than one column, and only row_num or column_num is used, INDEX returns an array of the entire row or column in the *array* argument.

- INDEX returns an array of values, i.e., the entire row or column if you set row_num or column_num to 0 (zero).

- INDEX returns a single value (at the intersection of row_num and column_num) if both arguments are used.

- To return several values, enter the formula in the first cell and press **Enter**. Excel will spill the return values to other cells.

Example 1

In the following example, we can return the sum of the entire row for Q1. We can return this result by combining the INDEX and SUM functions.

The example uses a drop-down list in cell H3 to select the row. The formula in cell I3 references H3 for the row_num argument.

When we select **1** in H3, we're setting the row_num to 1. The column_num argument is 0 (zero) in the formula, specifying that we want to return all the values in the range B4:E4.

=SUM(INDEX(B4:E7,H3,0))

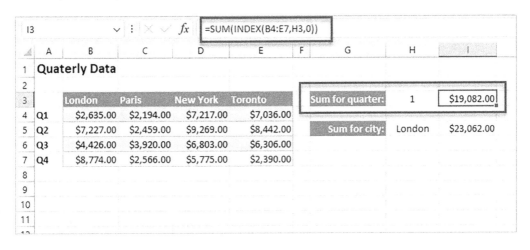

Example 2

In the following example, we want to return the sum of an entire column, for instance, B4:B7. We can achieve this result by combining the INDEX, SUM, and XMATCH functions.

=SUM(INDEX(B4:E7,0,XMATCH(H5,B3:E3)))

I5				fx	=SUM(INDEX(B4:E7,0,XMATCH(H5,B3:E3)))				
	A	B	C	D	E	F	G	H	I
1	Quaterly Data								
2									
3		London	Paris	New York	Toronto		Sum for quarter:	1	$19,082.00
4	Q1	$2,635.00	$2,194.00	$7,217.00	$7,036.00				
5	Q2	$7,227.00	$2,459.00	$9,269.00	$8,442.00		Sum for city:	London	$23,062.00
6	Q3	$4,426.00	$3,920.00	$6,803.00	$6,306.00				
7	Q4	$8,774.00	$2,566.00	$5,775.00	$2,390.00				
8									
9									
10									

Formula explanation

=SUM(INDEX(B4:E7,0,XMATCH(H5,B3:E3)))

The INDEX function in the formula uses a nested XMATCH to return its column_num argument:

XMATCH(H5,B3:E3)

The XMATCH function uses the value in cell H5 as its lookup_value. Its lookup_array is B3:E3 (the column headers with the city names). The match_mode is omitted as we want an exact match. XMATCH returns a number corresponding to the column that matches the lookup value. In this example, the lookup value is **London**, so XMATCH returns **1**.

Thus, for the INDEX function, the array is B4:E7; the row_num is 0, meaning we want to return all rows; and the column_num is 1, which returns every value in the first column of the range B4:E7.

The SUM function then sums all values returned from the first column.

INDEX Function - Reference Form

The reference form of the INDEX function returns the value of the cell at the intersection of a row and column. The reference argument can be made up of non-contiguous ranges, and you can pick which range to search using the area_num argument.

Syntax

=INDEX(reference, row_num,[col_num],[area_num])

Arguments

Argument	Description
reference	Required. A reference to one or more ranges. If you are entering more than one range, enclose this argument in parentheses. For example, INDEX((A1:B10,D1:D10),3,4).
row_num	Required. The row number in *reference* from which to return a value. If row_num is omitted, column_num is required.
column_num	Optional. Selects the column in the *array* argument from which to return a value. If column_num is omitted, row_num is required.
area_num	Optional. Selects a range in *reference* from which the intersection of *row_num* and *column_num* will be returned. The areas are numbered 1, 2, 3, etc. If area_num is omitted, the default, 1, is used. The areas need to be on the same worksheet.

Remarks

- If you specify areas in *reference* that are not on the same worksheet as each other, the function will return an error (#VALUE!). If you need to use ranges on different worksheets, it is recommended that you use the array form of INDEX and use another function to generate the range that makes up the array. For example, you could use the CHOOSE function to specify the ranges.

- If each area in *reference* contains only one row or column, the row_num or column_num argument is optional. For example, use INDEX(reference, column_num) for a single-row reference.

- *row_num* and *column_num* must point to a cell within *reference,* or the function will return a #REF! error.

Example

In this example, we have four named ranges making up the *reference* argument:

Reference	Range name	Area_num
B6:E9	Year1	1
H6:K9	Year2	2
B13:E16	Year3	3
H13:K16	Year4	4

To return a value from one of these ranges, we specify the range with a *area_num.* The ranges are numbered by order of entry, starting from 1.

Year1 = 1; Year2 = 2; Year3 = 3; Year4 = 4

In the following formula, we want to return the value in Year 4, Q3, for Toronto.

=INDEX((Year1,Year2,Year3,Year4),3,4,J2)

A cell reference, J2, is used for the *area_num* so that the value can be easily changed on the worksheet to point to a different range when needed.

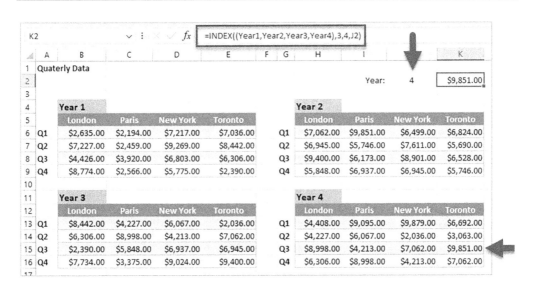

The formula returns **$9,851.00** from the fourth range in the third row and fourth column.

The INDEX function is most useful when combined with other functions like XMATCH.

Finding Matches with INDEX and XMATCH

In the example below, we want to identify the sales amount for a Sales Rep for a given quarter. The combination of INDEX/XMATCH/XMATCH enables us to perform a simultaneous vertical and horizontal lookup.

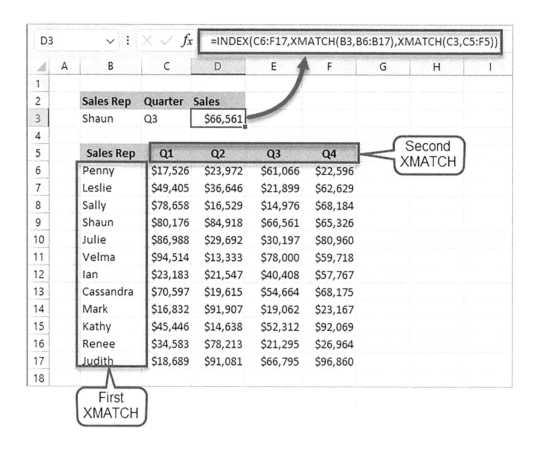

Formula explanation:

=INDEX(C6:F17,XMATCH(B3,B6:B17),XMATCH(C3,C5:F5))

The INDEX function has three arguments. The first argument is the range C6:F17. The first XMATCH function represents *row_num,* while the second XMATCH function represents the *column_num* argument.

The first XMATCH function returns **4**, which is the relative position of "Shaun" in range B6:B17, while the second XMATCH function returns **3**, which is the relative position of "Q3" in range C5:F5.

You can use the **Evaluate Formula** command (on the **Formulas** tab) to step through the formula and see the results at each evaluation stage until it gets to the final arguments used to execute the INDEX function. The image below shows that the *row_num* and *column_num* arguments evaluate to 4 and 3.

=INDEX(C6:F17,4,3)

Evaluate Formula	? X
Reference:	Evaluation:
Sheet3!$D$3	= INDEX($C$6:$F$17,4,3)

To show the result of the underlined expression, click Evaluate. The most recent result appears italicized.

| Evaluate | Step In | Step Out | Close |

Manipulating Columns and Rows

The functions in this category enable you to select and return several columns or rows in your specified order. You can also transpose columns or rows.

CHOOSECOLS Function

The CHOOSECOLS function returns the specified columns from a range in the order specified in the arguments. This function enables you to select a subset of columns or rearrange their order. You can use CHOOSECOLS to return an array as an argument in another formula.

Syntax

=CHOOSECOLS(array,col_num1,[col_num2],...)

Arguments

Arguments	Description
array	Required. The range or array that has the columns you want to return.
col_num1	Required. A number representing the first column to return from the range specified in *array*.
[col_num2], ...	Optional. A number representing an additional column to return. You can have several optional columns, for example, col_num3, col_num4, col_num5, etc.

Remarks

- Excel returns a #VALUE error if any of the col_num arguments exceeds the number of columns in the array.

- Excel returns a #VALUE error if any of the col_num arguments is 0.

Example 1

The formula below selects columns 2 and 4 from the range B2:E17.

=CHOOSECOLS(B2:E17,1,4)

▲	A	B	C	D	E	F	G	H
1	**Sales by Quarter**							
2		**QTR1**	**QTR2**	**QTR3**	**QTR4**		QTR1	QTR4
3	Chai	$672.00	$921.00	$344.00	$131.00		$672.00	$131.00
4	Beer	$966.00	$595.00	$136.00	$416.00		$966.00	$416.00
5	Coffee	$442.00	$564.00	$570.00	$427.00		$442.00	$427.00
6	Green Tea	$163.00	$284.00	$801.00	$713.00		$163.00	$713.00
7	Tea	$744.00	$282.00	$169.00	$142.00		$744.00	$142.00
8	Chocolate Biscuits Mix	$592.00	$104.00	$449.00	$652.00		$592.00	$652.00
9	Scones	$917.00	$814.00	$796.00	$593.00		$917.00	$593.00
10	Brownie Mix	$502.00	$270.00	$614.00	$313.00		$502.00	$313.00
11	Cake Mix	$555.00	$384.00	$250.00	$612.00		$555.00	$612.00
12	Granola	$555.00	$807.00	$244.00	$856.00		$555.00	$856.00
13	Hot Cereal	$770.00	$916.00	$858.00	$288.00		$770.00	$288.00
14	Chocolate	$258.00	$765.00	$578.00	$900.00		$258.00	$900.00
15	Fruit Cocktail	$552.00	$118.00	$335.00	$366.00		$552.00	$366.00
16	Pears	$763.00	$509.00	$374.00	$368.00		$763.00	$368.00
17	Peaches	$199.00	$998.00	$200.00	$264.00		$199.00	$264.00
18								
19								

G2 : =CHOOSECOLS(B2:E17,1,4)

Example 2 – Rearrange columns with CHOOSECOLS

The following example combines VLOOKUP and CHOOSECOLS to perform left lookups. By default, VLOOKUP is limited to only being able to perform right lookups, but we can use CHOOSECOLS to rearrange the columns so that our formula performs left lookups.

=VLOOKUP(B3,CHOOSECOLS(E3:F47,2,1),2,FALSE)

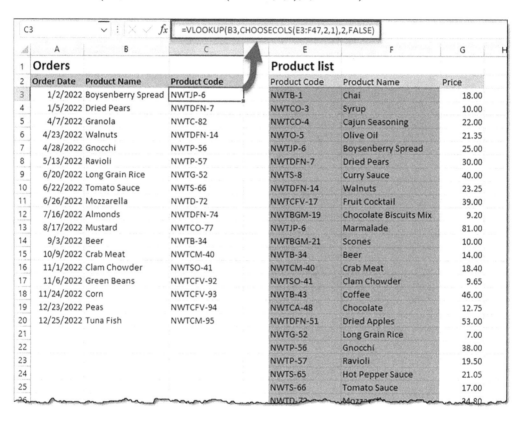

Formula explanation:

=VLOOKUP(B3,CHOOSECOLS(E3:F47,2,1),2,FALSE)

The formula reverses the order of the columns, placing column E to the right of column F with the following:

CHOOSECOLS(E3:F47,2,1).

The nested function has the following arguments:
- array = E3:F47
- col_num1 = 2
- col_num2 = 1

The formula returns an array with the first column as F3:F47 and the second column as E3:E47. Hence, VLOOKUP can now look up values in the first column (F3:F47) and return values from the second column, E3:E47.

See the section on VLOOKUP for a more detailed explanation of the function.

CHOOSEROWS Function

The CHOOSEROWS function returns several rows in the specified order from a range. This function is useful for returning an array as an argument in another formula.

Syntax

=CHOOSEROWS(array,row_num1,[row_num2],...)

Arguments

Argument	Description
array	Required. The range or array with the rows you want to return.
row_num1	Required. An integer representing the first row to return from the range specified in array.
[row_num2], ...	Optional. An integer representing an additional row to return. You can return several additional rows, for example, row_num3, row_num4, row_num5, etc.

Remarks

- Excel returns a #VALUE error if any of the row_num arguments exceeds the number of columns in the array.

- Excel returns a #VALUE error if any of the row_num arguments is 0.

Example 1

The following formula selects the first, fourth, and tenth rows from the array A2:C14.

=CHOOSEROWS(A2:C14,1,4,10)

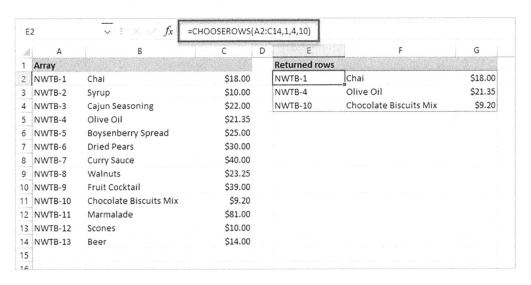

Example 2

The following formula selects the last three rows in reverse order from the array A2:C14 by using negative numbers for the row_num arguments. -1 returns the last row in the array, -2 returns the second to the last, and so on.

=CHOOSEROWS(A2:C14,-1,-2,-3)

	E2				fx	=CHOOSEROWS(A2:C14,-1,-2,-3)		
	A	B	C	D	E		F	G
1	Array				Returned rows			
2	NWTB-1	Chai	$18.00		NWTB-13	Beer		$14.00
3	NWTB-2	Syrup	$10.00		NWTB-12	Scones		$10.00
4	NWTB-3	Cajun Seasoning	$22.00		NWTB-11	Marmalade		$81.00
5	NWTB-4	Olive Oil	$21.35					
6	NWTB-5	Boysenberry Spread	$25.00					
7	NWTB-6	Dried Pears	$30.00					
8	NWTB-7	Curry Sauce	$40.00					
9	NWTB-8	Walnuts	$23.25					
10	NWTB-9	Fruit Cocktail	$39.00					
11	NWTB-10	Chocolate Biscuits Mix	$9.20					
12	NWTB-11	Marmalade	$81.00					
13	NWTB-12	Scones	$10.00					
14	NWTB-13	Beer	$14.00					
15								

Using an Array Constant

You can use an array constant in place of an argument to return multiple rows and simplify the formula. An array constant is a set of values enclosed in curly brackets {} often used in formulas to create or manipulate several values simultaneously rather than a single value.

For example, {"apple","orange","pear"}.

Example 3

The following formula uses an array constant to specify the rows returned by CHOOSEROWS.

=CHOOSEROWS(A3:C12,{1,2,3})

Notice the array constant {1,2,3} takes up only one argument in the formula but returns three rows.

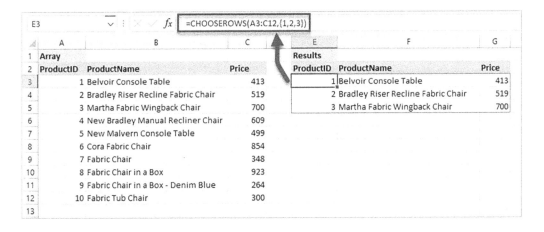

CHOOSE Function

The CHOOSE function allows you to use an index number to return a value from a list of arguments. The arguments can be values or cell references. You can use CHOOSE to select one out of a maximum of 254 values based on the index number.

CHOOSE is more useful when used in with another function in a formula. For example, you can use CHOOSE to rearrange columns in a list to perform left lookups with VLOOKUP.

Syntax

=CHOOSE(index_num, value1, [value2], ...)

Arguments

Argument	Description
index_num	Required. This argument specifies the value to be selected from the list. The value must be a number between 1 and 254. It can be a formula or a cell reference that returns a number between 1 and 254.
value1	Required. The first value is required. Values can be numbers, cell references, ranges, formulas, functions, or text.
[value2], ...	Optional. You can have up to 253 additional optional values.

Remarks

If the index_num argument is less than 1 or greater than the number of the last value in the list, CHOOSE returns a #VALUE! error. If index_num is a fraction, it will be truncated to the lowest integer.

Example 1

The CHOOSE function is most useful when used in combination with another function. For example, we can nest the CHOOSE function within the SUM function.

The example below has one SUM formula that can calculate the total of individual quarters. We just need to specify the quarter number to determine which quarter to calculate.

C20		fx	=SUM(CHOOSE(B20,B3:B17,C3:C17,D3:D17,E3:E17))			
	A	B	C	D	E	F	G
1	**Sales by Quarter**						
2		**QTR1**	**QTR2**	**QTR3**	**QTR4**		
3	Chai	$672.00	$921.00	$344.00	$131.00		
4	Beer	$966.00	$595.00	$136.00	$416.00		
5	Coffee	$442.00	$564.00	$570.00	$427.00		
6	Green Tea	$163.00	$284.00	$801.00	$713.00		
7	Tea	$744.00	$282.00	$169.00	$142.00		
8	Chocolate Biscuits Mix	$592.00	$104.00	$449.00	$652.00		
9	Scones	$917.00	$814.00	$796.00	$593.00		
10	Brownie Mix	$502.00	$270.00	$614.00	$313.00		
11	Cake Mix	$555.00	$384.00	$250.00	$612.00		
12	Granola	$555.00	$807.00	$244.00	$856.00		
13	Hot Cereal	$770.00	$916.00	$858.00	$288.00		
14	Chocolate	$258.00	$765.00	$578.00	$900.00		
15	Fruit Cocktail	$552.00	$118.00	$335.00	$366.00		
16	Pears	$763.00	$509.00	$374.00	$368.00		
17	Peaches	$199.00	$998.00	$200.00	$264.00		
18							
19							
20	CHOOSE QTR	4	$7,041.00				
21							

Formula explanation

The following formula is entered in cell C20:

=SUM(CHOOSE(B20,B3:B17,C3:C17,D3:D17,E3:E17))

The value in **B20** is **4**, which represents **QTR4**. So, the result returned by the formula is for the range E3:E17.

The CHOOSE function is first evaluated, and it returns the range E3:E17. The SUM function then sums up E3:E17 to provide the total for that quarter.

Of course, looking at the example above, it may appear that it would be easier to just sum up each quarter separately. However, there may be scenarios when we want to produce dynamic summaries by changing the target range.

Example 2 – Rearrange columns with CHOOSE

One limitation of VLOOKUP is that we can only return values in a column to the right of the lookup range. In the example below, the lookup range is F3:F47, and the return range is E3:E47. The return values are in a column to the left of the lookup column.

For example, imagine that we're not allowed to rearrange the columns of the original data. We can use the CHOOSE function to rearrange the columns for the table_array argument of VLOOKUP.

Applying the CHOOSE function to our formula produces the following:

=VLOOKUP(B3,CHOOSE({1,2},ProductNames,ProductCodes),2,FALSE)

Note that this formula uses two range names:

- ProductCodes = E3:E47
- ProductNames = F3:F47

> -Tip Use range names instead of absolute references, as they're easier to read in formulas.

| C3 | | ✓ : ✗ ✓ *fx* | =VLOOKUP(B3,CHOOSE({1,2},ProductNames,ProductCodes),2,FALSE) | | | |

	A	B	C	D	E	F	G
1	**Orders**				**Product list**		
2	**Order Date**	**Product Name**	**Product Code**		Product Code	Product Name	Price
3	01/02/2016	Boysenberry Spread	NWTJP-6		NWTB-1	Chai	18.00
4	01/05/2016	Dried Pears	NWTDFN-7		NWTCO-3	Syrup	10.00
5	04/07/2016	Granola	NWTC-82		NWTCO-4	Cajun Seasoning	22.00
6	04/23/2016	Walnuts	NWTDFN-14		NWTO-5	Olive Oil	21.35
7	04/28/2016	Gnocchi	NWTP-56		NWTJP-6	Boysenberry Spread	25.00
8	05/13/2016	Ravioli	NWTP-57		NWTDFN-7	Dried Pears	30.00
9	06/20/2016	Long Grain Rice	NWTG-52		NWTS-8	Curry Sauce	40.00
10	06/22/2016	Tomato Sauce	NWTS-66		NWTDFN-14	Walnuts	23.25
11	06/26/2016	Mozzarella	NWTD-72		NWTCFV-17	Fruit Cocktail	39.00
12	07/16/2016	Almonds	NWTDFN-74		NWTBGM-19	Chocolate Biscuits Mix	9.20
13	08/17/2016	Mustard	NWTCO-77		NWTJP-6	Marmalade	81.00
14	09/03/2016	Beer	NWTB-34		NWTBGM-21	Scones	10.00
15	10/09/2016	Crab Meat	NWTCM-40		NWTB-34	Beer	14.00
16	11/01/2016	Clam Chowder	NWTSO-41		NWTCM-40	Crab Meat	18.40
17	11/06/2016	Green Beans	NWTCFV-92		NWTSO-41	Clam Chowder	9.65
18	11/24/2016	Corn	NWTCFV-93		NWTB-43	Coffee	46.00
19	12/23/2016	Peas	NWTCFV-94		NWTCA-48	Chocolate	12.75
20	12/25/2016	Tuna Fish	NWTCM-95		NWTDFN-51	Dried Apples	53.00
21					NWTG-52	Long Grain Rice	7.00
22					NWTP-56	Gnocchi	38.00
23					NWTP-57	Ravioli	19.50
24					NWTS-65	Hot Pepper Sauce	21.05
25					NWTS-66	Tomato Sauce	

CHOOSE column 2   CHOOSE column 1

Formula explanation:

=VLOOKUP(B3,CHOOSE({1,2},ProductNames,ProductCodes),2,FALSE)

Our table_array is E3:F47, and we want to return values in column E. We want a method in our formula that reverses the order of the columns, that is, put column E to the right of column F. The CHOOSE formula can do this:

CHOOSE({1,2},ProductNames,ProductCodes)

This formula has F3:F47 (ProductName) as the *value1* argument and E3:E47 (ProductCodes) as the *value2* argument. Both ranges are absolute references in the formula, as range names are absolute references by default.

The *index_num* argument of our CHOOSE function is an array constant {1,2}, which tells the function to return the data in the order *value1* and *value2*, that is, ProductNames before ProductCodes.

With the columns of *table_array* now rearranged by CHOOSE, VLOOKUP can now look up a value in ProductNames, and return a corresponding value in ProductCodes.

We can fill down the formula to populate the other cells in column C.

TRANSPOSE Function

The TRANSPOSE function enables you to transpose data in your worksheet. If you want to rotate data on your worksheet, you can use the Transpose option on the paste command. The TRANSPOSE function provides a way to perform the same task automatically with a formula. TRANSPOSE can be useful when you want to copy and transpose data from several ranges across different worksheets.

> **Tip** To manually copy and transpose a range as a one-off task, use the **Transpose** option on the **Paste** command (or the **Paste Special** dialog box).

Syntax

=TRANSPOSE(array)

Argument

Argument	Description
array	Required. The range of cells that you want to transpose.

Example:

In this example, we want to transpose the data in cells A1:B4 in the table below.

Follow the steps below to copy and transpose a range:

1. Click the top-left cell of the destination range.
2. In the formula bar, type **=TRANSPOSE(**
3. Select the source range on the worksheet with your mouse.
4. Enter the closing bracket.
5. Press **Enter**.

Excel transposes the data from the top-left of the destination cell and spills it to adjacent cells.

A7	⌄ ⋮ ✕ ✓ *fx* =TRANSPOSE(A1:B4)				
	A	B	C	D	E
1	QTR1	$2,000.00			
2	QTR2	$3,000.00			
3	QTR3	$1,400.00			
4	QTR4	$5,000.00			
5					
6					
7	QTR1	QTR2	QTR3	QTR4	
8	2000	3000	1400	5000	
9					

📝 **Note** If you're using a standalone version of Excel before Excel 2021, you need to select all cells needed for the result and then press **CTRL+SHIFT+ENTER** to paste the result of the formula.

COLUMNS and ROWS Functions

The COLUMNS function returns the number of columns in an array or range. The ROWS function returns the number of rows in an array or range. These two functions are often used in formulas where you need to return the number of columns or rows in a specified range as an argument of another function.

As these two functions are very similar, this section covers them simultaneously.

Syntax

=COLUMNS(array)

=ROWS(array)

Argument	Description
array	Required. An array or a reference to a range you want to count.

Example

The following example counts the number of rows and columns in a range.

The formulas used to get the count are:

=COLUMNS(A1:E23)

=ROWS(A1:E23)

⬜	A	B	C	D	E	F	G	H	I
1	$2,635	$7,227	$4,426	$8,774	$9,829			Count	Formula Text
2	$2,194	$2,459	$3,920	$2,566	$4,894		Rows:	23	=ROWS(A1:E23)
3	$7,217	$9,269	$6,803	$5,775	$4,857		Columns:	5	=COLUMNS(A1:E23)
4	$7,036	$8,442	$6,306	$2,390	$7,734				
5	$4,408	$4,227	$8,998	$5,848	$3,375				
6	$9,095	$6,067	$4,213	$6,937	$9,024				
7	$9,879	$2,036	$7,062	$6,945	$9,400				
8	$6,692	$3,063	$9,851	$5,746	$6,173				
9	$3,513	$4,434	$6,499	$7,611	$8,901				
10	$4,032	$4,280	$6,824	$5,690	$6,528				
11	$7,217	$9,269	$6,803	$5,775	$4,857				
12	$7,036	$8,442	$6,306	$2,390	$7,734				

Returning Cell Information

The functions under this category enable you to create formulas that return information about a cell. For example, the formula in the cell or its reference.

FORMULATEXT Function

The FORMULATEXT function enables you to display the formula from one cell in another cell in your worksheet. This function is useful for identifying errors in your syntax or comparing different formulas side by side. Instead of only checking your formulas one at a time by clicking on each cell, you can use FORMULATEXT to reveal the formulas in several cells simultaneously.

Syntax

FORMULATEXT(reference)

Argument

Argument	Description
reference	Required. A reference to a cell in the current workbook or another open workbook.

Remarks

FORMULATEXT will return the #N/A error if:

- The cell used as the reference argument does not contain a formula.
- The reference argument is in an external workbook that is not open.
- The formula can't be displayed due to worksheet protection.

If the reference argument points to more than one cell, for example, a range, FORMULATEXT will return the value in the upper leftmost cell in the range.

Example

In this example, we have some values in column A. In column B, we have several formulas to aggregate column A values. The worksheet uses FORMULATEXT to display the formulas in column C.

C2		fx	=FORMULATEXT(B2)	
	A	B	C	D
1	Values	Aggregate results	Formula text	
2	$18.00	$181.35	=SUM(A2:A9)	
3	$10.00	$22.67	=AVERAGE(A2:A9)	
4	$22.00	8	=COUNT(A2:A9)	
5	$21.35	$40.00	=MAX(A2:A9)	
6	$25.00	$10.00	=MIN(A2:A9)	
7	$30.00	$21.68	=MEDIAN(A2:A9)	
8	$15.00			
9	$40.00			
10				

ADDRESS Function

You can use the ADDRESS function to return the address of a cell in a worksheet when you provide the row and column numbers as arguments. For example, =ADDRESS(4,6) returns $F$4. This function is useful when you need to return the address of a cell in your formula.

Syntax

=ADDRESS(row_num, column_num, [abs_num], [a1], [sheet_text])

Arguments

Argument	Description
row_num	Required. A number that specifies the row number to use in the cell reference.
column_num	Required. A number that specifies the column number to use in the cell reference.
abs_num	Optional. Specifies the reference type to return, e.g., absolute, relative, or mixed reference. The default is Absolute reference, which will be used if abs_num is omitted.
	Argument values
	1 (or omitted) = Absolute reference
	2 = Mixed reference. Absolute row, relative column
	3 = Mixed reference. Relative row, absolute column
	4 = Relative reference
a1	Optional. A logical value that specifies whether to use the A1 or R1C1 style of reference. TRUE is A1, and FALSE is R1C1. If this argument is omitted, A1 is used.
sheet_text	Optional. A string specifying the name of the worksheet from which to get the cell reference. To be used when connecting to an external sheet. If this argument is omitted, the current sheet is used.

> **Note** In Excel, A1 referencing means columns are labeled alphabetically and rows numerically. R1C1 referencing means both columns and rows are labeled numerically.

The A1 reference style is the default and the recommendation for most occasions. However, if you need to change the reference style, click **File** > **Options** > **Formulas**. Under **Working with formulas**, check or uncheck the **R1C1 reference style** checkbox. The default reference style is A1, so R1C1 should be unchecked by default.

Examples

Example 1

Formula:	=ADDRESS(2,4)
Description:	Absolute reference in the current sheet.
Result:	$D$2

Example 2

Formula:	=ADDRESS(2,4,2)
Description:	Mixed reference. Absolute row; relative column.
Result:	D$2

Example 3

Formula:	=ADDRESS(2,4,2,FALSE)
Description:	Mixed reference. Absolute row; relative column using the R1C1 reference style.
Result:	R2C[4]

Example 4

Formula:	=ADDRESS(2,4,1,FALSE,"[Book2]Sheet1")
Description:	An absolute reference to another workbook (Book2) and worksheet.
Result:	[Book2]Sheet1!R2C4

Example 5

Formula:	=ADDRESS(2,4,1,FALSE,"Accounts sheet")
Description:	An absolute reference to another worksheet.
Result:	'Accounts sheet'!R2C4

Filtering and Sorting Ranges

The dynamic array functions in this section allow you to select data from lists and return arrays that are filtered or sorted without changing the source data.

UNIQUE Function

Excel's UNIQUE function is a dynamic array function that returns a list of unique values in an array or range. UNIQUE returns an array, which spills across the required range if it's the final output of a formula. When you press ENTER, Excel will dynamically create the required sized range for the output.

Note that you can use the **Remove Duplicates** command button in Excel to create unique rows in a list manually. However, UNIQUE comes in handy when you need to return an array of unique values in a formula or to create a dynamic list of unique values without changing the original data source.

Syntax

=UNIQUE(array,[by_col],[exactly_once])

Arguments

Argument	Description
array	Required. The range or array from which to return unique values.
by_col	Optional. A logical value specifying how to perform the comparison.
	TRUE = compare columns against each other.
	FALSE (or omitted) = compare rows against each other.
exactly_once	Optional. This argument is a logical value to indicate whether to return rows/columns that only occur once in array.
	TRUE = return values that occur only once in the range/array.
	FALSE (or omitted) = return all distinct values (i.e., eliminate duplicates).

Example

The following example uses Excel's UNIQUE to generate a list of unique states from the range B2:B19. A lookup list like this can be used as the data source for a dropdown list somewhere else in the worksheet. Dynamically generating the list saves you from manually creating the lookup list.

Formula explanation

=SORT(UNIQUE(B2:B19,FALSE,FALSE))

The range B2:B19 is the array argument. The by_col and exactly_once arguments are FALSE, meaning the formula returns all unique values, i.e., removes duplicates. The result is displayed in the range E2:E12. Note that the formula uses the SORT function to sort the returned array in alphabetical order.

E2		fx	=SORT(UNIQUE(B2:B19,FALSE,FALSE))	

	A	B	C	D	E	F
1	Salesperson	State	Sales		States - Unique	
2	Hill, Virginia	Minnesota(MN)	$4,061		Arizona(AZ)	
3	Johnson, Cheryl	Texas(TX)	$2,746		Georgia(GA)	
4	Griffin, Ruth	Kentucky(KY)	$5,183		Illinois(IL)	
5	Morris, Andrea	Minnesota(MN)	$5,048		Kentucky(KY)	
6	Walker, Steven	Georgia(GA)	$3,851		Louisiana(LA)	
7	Hall, Ruby	Louisiana(LA)	$4,562		Massachusetts(MA)	
8	Rogers, Marilyn	Kentucky(KY)	$6,942		Minnesota(MN)	
9	Scott, Amanda	Georgia(GA)	$5,141		Mississippi(MS)	
10	Taylor, Christina	Mississippi(MS)	$2,634		Pennsylvania(PA)	
11	Diaz, Jerry	Texas(TX)	$1,149		Texas(TX)	
12	Russell, Jack	Texas(TX)	$6,586		Washington(WA)	
13	Mitchell, Linda	Washington(WA)	$5,473			
14	Sanchez, Shawn	Texas(TX)	$1,971			
15	Campbell, Dorothy	Pennsylvania(PA)	$6,027			
16	Ross, Kimberly	Illinois(IL)	$4,670			
17	Thompson, Raymond	Massachusetts(MA)	$2,018			
18	Simmons, Shirley	Texas(TX)	$1,270			
19	Morgan, Gary	Arizona(AZ)	$5,224			
20						
21						

FILTER Function

The FILTER function is a dynamic array function that filters and returns an array based on the specified criteria. You can filter a range using the **Filter** command on the Excel ribbon. However, the FILTER function is useful when supplying the range as an argument inside a formula to display the result as an array in a different range. FILTER will return several values, which will spill across the cells required to hold the result when you enter the formula and press ENTER.

Syntax

=FILTER(array,include,[if_empty])

Arguments

Argument	Description
array	Required. The range you want to filter. This can be a row of values, a column of values, or several rows and columns of values.
include	Required. A Boolean array or an expression specifying the criteria that returns a Boolean array. For example, A2:A10="Apples".
[if_empty]	Optional. You can specify a string value to return if the filter returns nothing. For example, "No data".

Remarks

- FILTER will return a #CALC! error if the return value is empty, as Excel does not currently support empty arrays. To avoid this error, if there is a possibility that your formula will return no records, use the if_empty argument to specify a value to return in place of the error.

- FILTER will return an error (#N/A, #VALUE, etc.) if any value in the criteria range is an error or cannot be converted to a Boolean value with the expression in the *include* argument.

- The *include* argument should be a Boolean array or an expression that returns a Boolean array whose height or width is the same as the array argument.

Example

The example below has a list of sales data in the range A3:D50. On the right of the worksheet, we want to view a subset of sales data filtered by product category.

We can combine FILTER and CHOOSECOLS to achieve the desired result as in the formula below.

=FILTER(CHOOSECOLS(A3:D50,1,2,4),C3:C50=G3,"No data")

	F6				f_x	=FILTER(CHOOSECOLS(A3:D50,1,2,4),C3:C50=G3,"No data")			
	A	B	C	D		F	G	H	
1	Sales					Filtered by product category			
2	Salesperson	Product	Category	Price					
3	Ross Grant	Cora Fabric Chair	Chair	$706		Enter Category:	Sofa		
4	Jan Kotas	Lukah Leather Chair	Chair	$1,049					
5	Mae Stevens	Habitat Oken Console Table	Table	$1,706		Product	Product	Price	
6	Jesse Garza	Tessa Fabric Sofa	Sofa	$1,213		Jesse Garza	Tessa Fabric Sofa	$1,213	
7	Ross Grant	Harley Fabric Cuddle Chair	Chair	$1,317		Mae Stevens	Tessa Fabric Sofa	$1,213	
8	Jan Kotas	Windsor 2 Seater Cuddle Chair	Chair	$1,687		Ross Grant	Trieste Leather Sofa	$628	
9	Mae Stevens	Fabric Tub Chair	Chair	$1,060		Jesse Garza	Tessa Fabric Sofa	$1,213	
10	Laura Giussani	Verona 1 Shelf Table	Table	$1,265		Ross Grant	Tessa Fabric Sofa	$1,213	
11	Ross Grant	Floral Fabric Tub Chair	Chair	$915					
12	Jan Kotas	Fabric Chair in a Box	Box	$856					
13	Mae Stevens	Slimline Console Table	Table	$762					
14	Loren Pratt	Martha Fabric Wingback Chair	Chair	$883					
15	Loren Pratt	Slimline Console Table	Table	$626					
16	Loren Pratt	Fabric Wingback Chair	Chair	$1,786					
17	Loren Pratt	Fabric Chair in a Box	Box	$888					
18	Loren Pratt	Verona Chair in a Box	Box	$765					
19	Robert Zare	Cora Fabric Chair	Chair	$1,772					
20	Jesse Garza	Fabric Wingback Chair	Chair	$773					
21	Mae Stevens	Tessa Fabric Sofa	Sofa	$1,213					

Formula explanation

=FILTER(CHOOSECOLS(A3:D50,1,2,4),C3:C50=G3,"No data")

This formula is in two parts. The first part uses CHOOSECOLS to return all values in columns 1, 2, and 4 from the range A3:D50.

The second part of the formula uses the FILTER function to filter the result using the expression **C3:C50=G3**. This expression is the *include* argument for the FILTER function. It uses the criteria in cell G3 to filter the values in the range C3:C50 to return rows where the product category matches the criteria.

The value in the *if_empty* argument ensures the formula returns "No data" instead of an error for instances where no results match the entered criteria.

SORT Function

The SORT function is a dynamic array function that takes in an array and returns a sorted list based on the sort_index and sort_order you have specified. SORT will spill the result across the required range. The SORT function is more useful for sorting an array as an argument. To sort data directly on the worksheet, use the SORTBY function, which supports multi-level sorting.

Syntax:

=SORT(array,[sort_index],[sort_order],[by_col])

Arguments

Argument	Description
array	Required. The range or array to sort.
sort_index	Optional. A number that specifies the row or column within the array to sort by. The default is 1 if omitted.
sort_order	Optional. The sort order to use.
	1 = ascending (default).
	-1 =descending.
	If omitted, the default is ascending.
by_col	Optional. A logical value to indicate whether to sort by column or by row.
	FALSE = sort by row (default)
	TRUE = sort by column
	If omitted, the default is FALSE, i.e., sort by row.

Example

In the following example, we want to return records filtered by State to show the best-performing salespeople first. The following formula combines the SORT and FILTER functions to achieve the desired result.

=SORT(FILTER(A3:C20,B3:B20=F1),3,-1)

E5				fx	=SORT(FILTER(A3:C20,B3:B20=F1),3,-1)		
	A	B	C	D	E	F	G
1	Array				Enter State:	TX	
2	Salesperson	State	Sales				
3	Hill, Virginia	MN	$4,061		Filtered list		
4	Johnson, Cheryl	TX	$2,746		Salesperson	State	Sales
5	Griffin, Ruth	KY	$5,183		Russell, Jack	TX	$6,586
6	Morris, Andrea	MN	$5,048		Johnson, Cheryl	TX	$2,746
7	Walker, Steven	GA	$3,851		Sanchez, Shawn	TX	$1,971
8	Hall, Ruby	LA	$4,562		Simmons, Shirley	TX	$1,270
9	Rogers, Marilyn	KY	$6,942		Diaz, Jerry	TX	$1,149
10	Scott, Amanda	GA	$5,141				
11	Taylor, Christina	MS	$2,634				
12	Diaz, Jerry	TX	$1,149				
13	Russell, Jack	TX	$6,586				
14	Mitchell, Linda	WA	$5,473				
15	Sanchez, Shawn	TX	$1,971				
16	Campbell, Dorothy	PA	$6,027				
17	Ross, Kimberly	IL	$4,670				
18	Thompson, Raymond	MA	$2,018				
19	Simmons, Shirley	TX	$1,270				
20	Morgan, Gary	AZ	$5,224				
21							

Formula explanation:

=SORT(FILTER(A3:C20,B3:B20=F1),3,-1)

The above formula has A3:C20 as the array from which we want to extract a filtered and sorted list.

The FILTER function has **B3:B20=F1** as its *include* argument. This expression filters the data in cells A3:C20 and returns only rows where the State matches the value entered in cell F1.

The SORT function's sort_index argument is **3**, indicating the formula uses the third column (Sales) for the sort. The sort_order is **-1**, which sorts the data in descending order.

The result is a list filtered by state and sorted in descending order by sales.

SORTBY Function

The SORTBY function sorts the values of a range or array based on specified 'sort by' ranges and sort orders. SORTBY is an array function and spills the result across the required range. The 'sort by' range does not necessarily need to be part of the source range but must have the same number of rows as the source range. You can perform a multi-level sort by providing additional pairs of by_array and sort_order arguments.

Syntax

=SORTBY(array, by_array1, [sort_order1], [by_array2, sort_order2],...)

Arguments

Argument	Description
array	Required. The range or array to sort.
by_array1	Required. The range or array to sort by.
[sort_order1]	Optional. The sort order to use.
	1 = ascending
	-1 = descending
	If omitted, the default is ascending.
[by_array2, sort_order2],...	Optional. Additional pairs of by_array/sort_order arguments to sort the array by more than one field.

Remarks

- All range/array arguments must be the same size.
- SORTBY will return a #VALUE! error if you enter a sort order argument that's not 1 or -1. If you omit the sort order argument, Excel will use ascending order.

Example 1

In the following example, we use SORTBY to sort and return the range B3:C20 by the **State** and **Sales** amount (B3:B20 and C3:C20). So, the formula has a two-level sort. The sorted data is displayed in cell E20:F20.

=SORTBY(B3:C20,B3:B20,1,C3:C20,-1)

	fx	=SORTBY(B3:C20,B3:B20,1,C3:C20,-1)				

	A	B	C	D	E	F
1	Array				Sorted Result	
2	Salesperson	State	Sales		State	Sales
3	Hill, Virginia	Minnesota(MN)	$4,061		Arizona(AZ)	$5,224
4	Johnson, Cheryl	Texas(TX)	$2,746		Georgia(GA)	$5,141
5	Griffin, Ruth	Kentucky(KY)	$5,183		Georgia(GA)	$3,851
6	Morris, Andrea	Minnesota(MN)	$5,048		Illinois(IL)	$4,670
7	Walker, Steven	Georgia(GA)	$3,851		Kentucky(KY)	$6,942
8	Hall, Ruby	Louisiana(LA)	$4,562		Kentucky(KY)	$5,183
9	Rogers, Marilyn	Kentucky(KY)	$6,942		Louisiana(LA)	$4,562
10	Scott, Amanda	Georgia(GA)	$5,141		Massachusetts(MA)	$2,018
11	Taylor, Christina	Mississippi(MS)	$2,634		Minnesota(MN)	$5,048
12	Diaz, Jerry	Texas(TX)	$1,149		Minnesota(MN)	$4,061
13	Russell, Jack	Texas(TX)	$6,586		Mississippi(MS)	$2,634
14	Mitchell, Linda	Washington(WA)	$5,473		Pennsylvania(PA)	$6,027
15	Sanchez, Shawn	Texas(TX)	$1,971		Texas(TX)	$6,586
16	Campbell, Dorothy	Pennsylvania(PA)	$6,027		Texas(TX)	$2,746
17	Ross, Kimberly	Illinois(IL)	$4,670		Texas(TX)	$1,971
18	Thompson, Raymond	Massachusetts(MA)	$2,018		Texas(TX)	$1,270
19	Simmons, Shirley	Texas(TX)	$1,270		Texas(TX)	$1,149
20	Morgan, Gary	Arizona(AZ)	$5,224		Washington(WA)	$5,473
21						

Formula explanation

=SORTBY(B3:C20,B3:B20,1,C3:C20,-1)

This formula has B3:C20 as the source array. B3:B20 is the first by_array (i.e., sort by) argument, and its sort order is 1 (ascending). The second by_array argument is C3:C20, and its sort order is -1 (descending).

The result is a list sorted by state alphabetically, then sales, in descending order. Thus, for each state, you'll see the highest sales first.

Chapter 3

Logical Functions

This chapter covers functions that enable you to:

- Select which statement to execute based on the result of a logical test.

- Check that multiple conditions are met with nested functions before executing a statement.

- Check that at least one of several conditions is met before executing a statement.

- Identify values in a list and provide replacement values.

- Trap errors in formulas and return a user-friendly message or a meaningful value.

The logical functions in Excel can be found by clicking the Logical command button on the Formulas tab of the Ribbon. A logical function requires a logical test before carrying out one evaluation from several options. If the test evaluates to TRUE, it executes one statement, and if the test is FALSE, it executes a different statement. A statement can be a calculation, a value, a string, or even another function. Logical functions can be nested, enabling you to perform multiple logical tests before executing the statement.

Creating Conditional Formulas

Logical functions allow you to create conditional formulas that can perform logical tests before returning a value based on the test result.

IF Function

The IF function is one of the popular functions in Excel used to create conditional formulas. The IF function allows you to perform a logical test (using comparison operators) that evaluates to TRUE or FALSE. The function executes one statement if the test is TRUE and another statement if the test is FALSE.

Syntax:

=IF(logical_test, value_if_true, [value_if_false])

Arguments

Argument	Description
logical_test	Required. A value or expression that can evaluate to TRUE or FALSE.
value_if_true	Required. The value returned if the logical test is true.
value_if_false	Optional. The value returned if the logical test is false. If the logical test is FALSE and this argument is omitted, nothing happens.

In its simplest form, this is what the function says:

IF (something is TRUE, then do A, otherwise do B)

Thus, the IF function will return a different result for TRUE and FALSE.

Example 1

A common way the IF function is used is to determine whether or not a referenced cell has any value. If the result is 0, then it returns a blank cell.

In the example below, the formula calculating the total for **Jan** was entered in cell **F2** and filled down to populate the totals for **Feb** to **Dec.** Without the IF function, the worksheet would display $0 for the unpopulated months. We want the totals for the unpopulated months to be blank instead of $0, even with the formula in place.

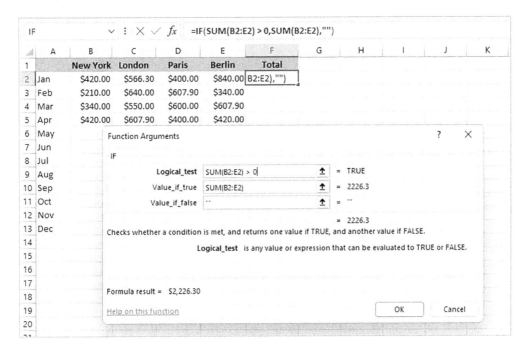

Thus, the formula for Jan in cell **F2** is:

=IF(SUM(B2:E2) > 0,SUM(B2:E2),"")

The IF function checks to see if the sum of Jan is greater than 0. If the test is TRUE, the formula returns the sum. Otherwise, it returns a blank string.
When we populate the other fields with the formula, we get the following:

F2					=IF(SUM(B2:E2) > 0,SUM(B2:E2),"")	
	A	B	C	D	E	F	G
1		New York	London	Paris	Berlin	Total	
2	Jan	$420.00	$566.30	$400.00	$840.00	$2,226.30	
3	Feb	$210.00	$640.00	$607.90	$340.00	$1,797.90	
4	Mar	$340.00	$550.00	$600.00	$607.90	$2,097.90	
5	Apr	$420.00	$607.90	$400.00	$420.00	$1,847.90	
6	May						
7	Jun						
8	Jul						
9	Aug						
10	Sep						
11	Oct						
12	Nov						
13	Dec						
14							

Example 2

In another example, we could use the results of an evaluation to return different values in our worksheet.

Let's say we have a budgeting sheet and want to use a "Status" column to report how the "Actual" amount compares to the "Budgeted" amount. We can use an IF formula to test whether the actual amount is greater than the budgeted amount. If **Actual** is greater than **Budgeted**, the formula enters **Over Budget**. Otherwise, it enters **Within Budget**.

D2			f_x	=IF(C2 > B2,"Over Budget", "Within Budget")			
	A	B	C	D	E	F	G
1	**Project**	**Budgeted**	**Actual**	**Status**			
2	Project1	$1,000.00	$900.00	Within Budget			
3	Project2	$2,000.00	$2,100.00	Over Budget			
4	Project3	$2,500.00	$1,500.00	Within Budget			
5	Project4	$2,300.00	$2,100.00	Within Budget			
6	Project5	$2,500.00	$2,300.00	Within Budget			
7	Project6	$1,200.00	$2,100.00	Over Budget			
8	Project7	$2,050.00	$2,030.00	Within Budget			
9	Project8	$5,000.00	$4,100.00	Within Budget			
10	Project9	$3,000.00	$2,100.00	Within Budget			
11							

=IF(C2 > B2,"Over Budget", "Within Budget")

The IF function checks to see if the value in C2 is greater than the value in B2. If it is, Excel returns **Over Budget**. Otherwise, it returns **Within Budget**.

Note that the example uses conditional formatting to automatically highlight the rows where the **Status** is **Over Budget**. You can apply conditional formatting to a range by selecting **Home** > **Conditional Formatting** > **New Rule**.

Conditional formatting is outside the scope of this book, but you can learn how to apply conditional formatting to your ranges in my *Excel 2022 Basics* book.

Example 3

In another example, we want to apply a **10%** promotional discount when **10 or more** items are purchased. We can use an IF formula to perform this conditional calculation.

E4				f_x	=IF(C4>=10,D4 - (D4 * 0.1),D4)	

	A	B	C	D	E	F
1	**Sales**					
2						
3	Product	Cost	Qty	Sub total	Total (with discount)	Formulatext
4	Beer	$1.50	15	$22.50	$20.25	=IF(C4>=10,D4 - (D4 * 0.1),D4)
5	Brownie Mix	$4.20	10	$42.00	$37.80	=IF(C5>=10,D5 - (D5 * 0.1),D5)
6	Cake Mix	$4.80	10	$48.00	$43.20	=IF(C6>=10,D6 - (D6 * 0.1),D6)
7	Chai	$1.80	10	$18.00	$16.20	=IF(C7>=10,D7 - (D7 * 0.1),D7)
8	Chocolate Biscuits Mix	$5.20	5	$26.00	$26.00	=IF(C8>=10,D8 - (D8 * 0.1),D8)
9	Coffee	$2.00	25	$50.00	$45.00	=IF(C9>=10,D9 - (D9 * 0.1),D9)
10	Green Tea	$2.00	50	$100.00	$90.00	=IF(C10>=10,D10 - (D10 * 0.1),D10)
11	Scones	$4.90	5	$24.50	$24.50	=IF(C11>=10,D11 - (D11 * 0.1),D11)
12	Tea	$1.30	20	$26.00	$23.40	=IF(C12>=10,D12 - (D12 * 0.1),D12)
13						
14						
15	*Apply a 10% discount if the quantity sold per item is 10 or more.					
16						

Formula explanation

=IF(C4>=10,D4 - (D4 * 0.1),D4)

The logical test checks if C4 (**Qty**) is greater than or equal to 10.

If the test is TRUE, the formula returns the sub-total minus 10%.

If the test is FALSE, the formula returns the sub-total.

We can use the fill handle of the cell to copy the formula to the other cells in the range E4:E12.

> **-Tip** The fill handle appears as a plus sign (+) when you hover your mouse pointer over the lower-right corner of the active cell.

Nested IF Functions

You can nest an IF function by inserting one IF function as an argument in another one. This formula is called a nested IF statement. You can nest up to seven IF statements. A nested IF statement might be required if you need to carry out more than one logical test in your formula.

Example 4

In the example below, we use a nested IF statement to test for three possible values and return a different result for each one.

We have a spreadsheet to record the score of exams, and we want to mark everything under 40 as FAIL, between 40 and 69 as CREDIT, and 70 or more as MERIT.

The formula would look like this:

=IF(B2 < 40, "FAIL",IF(B2 < 70,"CREDIT","MERIT"))

	A	B	C	D	E	F	G
C2			fx	=IF(B2 < 40, "FAIL",IF(B2 < 70,"CREDIT","MERIT"))			
1	**Student**	**Mark**	**Grade**				
2	Judith	67	CREDIT				
3	Paul	57	CREDIT				
4	David	51	CREDIT				
5	Randy	74	MERIT				
6	Mary	50	CREDIT				
7	Dorothy	30	FAIL				
8	Kimberly	95	MERIT				
9	Raymond	8	FAIL				
10	Shirley	30	FAIL				
11	Gary	57	CREDIT				
12	Lori	67	CREDIT				
13	Fred	81	MERIT				
14	Virginia	50	CREDIT				
15	Cheryl	30	FAIL				
16	Ruth	79	MERIT				

Formula explanation

=IF(B2 < 40, "FAIL",IF(B2 < 70,"CREDIT","MERIT"))

The first IF statement checks if B2 is less than 40. If TRUE, it returns "FAIL" and ends the evaluation there. If B2 < 40 is FALSE, the second IF test is executed.

The second IF function checks if B2 is less than 70. If true, it returns "CREDIT," and if false, it returns "MERIT."

> ☀-**Tip** The IFS function provides a better way of addressing multiple logical tests in one formula. As much as possible, use IFS instead of multiple nested IF statements. It is much cleaner and easier to read for multiple tests.

Example 5

In the following example, we want to calculate the commission paid to sales reps based on performance.

The formula calculates the following:

- If a sales rep generates $10,000 in sales AND 15 signups, they earn a 20% commission on their sales amount.

- If a sales rep generates $10,000 in sales OR 15 signups, they earn a 15% commission on their sales amount.

- If a sales rep generates less than $10,000 in sales and less than 15 signups, they earn a 10% commission on their sales amount.

The following formula returns the result we want:

=IF(D2 >= 10000,IF(E2 >= 15,D2*0.2,D2*0.15),IF(E2 >= 15,D2*0.15,D2*0.1))

fx | =IF(D2 >= 10000,IF(E2 >= 15,D2*0.2,D2*0.15),IF(E2 >= 15,D2*0.15,D2*0.1))

C	D	E	F	G	H
Sales rep	Sales	Signups	Commission		
Gilbert Higgins	$12,500	20	$2,500		
Clinton Bradley	$14,300	25	$2,860		
Bob Nash	$9,000	10	$900		
Lee Powers	$8,050	5	$805		
Mae Stevens	$5,000	7	$500		
Inez Griffith	$8,900	10	$890		
Theresa Hawkins	$7,900	10	$790		
Felix Jacobs	$6,000	17	$900		
Erik Lane	$11,000	18	$2,200		
Jesse Garza	$12,676	12	$1,901		
Alberta Fletcher	$13,163	14	$1,975		
Melody Mendoza	$8,795	20	$1,319		
Abraham Graves	$12,875	26	$2,575		
Van Sims	$6,646	16	$997		

Formula explanation

=IF(D2 >= 10000,IF(E2 >= 15,D2*0.2,D2*0.15),IF(E2 >= 15,D2*0.15,D2*0.1))

The outer IF function runs the test **D2 >= 10000** to check if D2 (Sales) is $10,000 or greater. If the result is TRUE, it runs the first nested IF function. If the result is FALSE, it runs the second nested IF function.

The first nested IF function checks whether signups are 15 or greater. If the result is TRUE, the formula returns 20% commission (D2*0.2) as its final result. If the test is FALSE, the formula returns a 15% commission (D2*0.15).

The second nested IF function is only executed if D2 is less than $10,000. It checks whether signups are 15 or greater. If the result is TRUE, the formula returns a 15% commission (D2*0.15) as its final result. If the test is false, the formula returns a 10% commission (D2*0.1).

Advanced IF Functions

An advanced IF function combines a logical function and a statistics or mathematics function. Advanced IF functions are covered in more detail in this book in the chapters for **Math Functions** and **Statistical Functions**. This section briefly examines some advanced IF functions you can use as one solution instead of combining two.

AVERAGEIF

Syntax:

=AVERAGEIF(range, criteria, [average_range])

This function returns the average (arithmetic mean) of numbers that meets the value you've entered as the criteria. The optional *average_range* argument allows you to specify another range for the values if it is separate from the one with the criteria.

Example:

=AVERAGEIF(A2:A20,"<2000")

The above formula calculates the average of all the values in the range A2:A20 that are greater than 2000.

AVERAGEIFS

Syntax:

=AVERAGEIFS(average_range,   criteria_range1,   criteria1,   [criteria_range2, criteria2], ...)

This function is similar to AVERAGEIF, but it allows you to specify multiple ranges and criteria in the arguments. You can specify up to 127 ranges and criteria.

COUNTIF

This function returns the count of the values in a range that meets the specified criteria.

Syntax:

=COUNTIF(range, criteria)

In its simplest form, this function says:

=COUNTIF(Where do you want to look?, What do you want to look for?)

Example:

=COUNTIF(A2:A10," New York")

This formula will return the count of the number of cells in A2:A10 with the value "New York."

COUNTIFS

=COUNTIFS(criteria_range1, criteria1, [criteria_range2, criteria2]...)

This function is like the COUNTIF function in that it returns a count based on a condition you specify. However, you can specify multiple ranges and criteria. You can specify up to 127 range/criteria pairs.

SUMIF

=SUMIF(range, criteria, [sum_range])

This function returns the sum of values in a range based on the criteria.

Example:

=SUMIF(A2:A10, ">10")

This formula returns the sum of all the values in cells A2:A10 that are greater than 10.

SUMIFS

Syntax:

SUMIFS(sum_range, criteria_range1, criteria1, [criteria_range2, criteria2], ...)

This function returns the sum of values that meet several criteria. You can specify up to 127 range/criteria pairs.

> **Note** All advanced IF functions mentioned above are covered in more detail elsewhere in this book. Check the table of contents for which chapter a function has been covered.

IFS Function

The IFS function enables you to carry out multiple logical tests and execute a statement corresponding to the first test that evaluates to TRUE. The tests need to be entered in the order you want the statements executed so that the right result is returned as soon as a test is passed. IFS was created as a better approach to nested IF statements, which can quickly become too complex.

Syntax

=IFS(logical_test1, value_if_true1, [logical_test2, value_if_true2], [logical_test3, value_if_true3],...)

Arguments

Argument	Description
logical_test1	Required. The condition that is being tested. It can evaluate to TRUE or FALSE.
value_if_true1	Required. The value returned if logical_test1 evaluates to TRUE.
logical_test2... logical_test127	Optional. An expression that evaluates to TRUE or FALSE. You can have up to 127 tests.
value_if_true2... value_if_true127	Optional. The value returned if a corresponding logical test evaluates to TRUE. You can have up to 127 values.

Remarks

The IFS function allows you to test up to 127 different tests. However, it is generally advised not to use too many tests with IF or IFS statements. Multiple tests need to be entered in the right order, and it can become too complex to update or maintain.

> **-Tip** As much as possible, use IFS instead of multiple nested IF statements. It is much easier to read when you have multiple conditions.

Example 1

In the example below, we use the IFS function to solve a problem we addressed earlier with nested IF statements. Notice how we don't need a nested function to achieve the same result.

In this problem, we want to assign grades to different ranges of exam scores.

Score and Grades
- 70 or above = MERIT
- 50 to 69 = CREDIT
- 40 to 49 = PASS
- less than 40 = FAIL

The following formula provides an ideal solution:

=IFS(B2>=70,"MERIT",B2>=50,"CREDIT", B2>=40,"PASS", B2<40,"FAIL")

C2				f_x	=IFS(B2>=70,"MERIT",B2>=50,"CREDIT", B2>=40,"PASS", B2<40,"FAIL")					

	A	B	C	D	E	F	G	H	I	J
1	**Student**	**Mark**	**Grade**							
2	Bruce	67	CREDIT							
3	Louis	57	CREDIT							
4	Earl	51	CREDIT							
5	Sean	74	MERIT							
6	Benjamin	50	CREDIT							
7	Joe	30	FAIL							
8	Shawn	95	MERIT							
9	Kenneth	8	FAIL							
10	Cynthia	30	FAIL							
11	Susan	57	CREDIT							
12	John	67	CREDIT							
13	Bruce	81	MERIT							
14	Louis	50	CREDIT							
15	Earl	30	FAIL							
16	Kenneth	79	MERIT							
17										

Formula explanation

=IFS(B2>=70,"MERIT",B2>=50,"CREDIT", B2>=40,"PASS", B2<40,"FAIL")

The IFS formula above has four logical tests in sequential order:

1. B2>=70,"MERIT"
2. B2>=50,"CREDIT"
3. B2>=40,"PASS"
4. B2<40,"FAIL"

B2 is a reference to the score. Each score is tested against each condition in sequential order. When a test returns TRUE, the corresponding grade is returned, and no further tests are carried out.

Example 2

In this example, we want to set different priority levels for re-ordering items depending on the number of items in stock.

Priority Level:
1. 5 or less = 1
2. 10 or less = 2
3. Less than 20 = 3

The formula we use to accomplish this task is:

=IFS(B2>20,"N/A",B2<=5,1, B2<=10,2, B2<20,3)

C2	∨ : ╳ ✓ fx	=IFS(B2>20,"N/A",B2<=5,1, B2<=10,2, B2<20,3)		
	A	B	C	D	E
1	Product	# In stock	Reorder Priority		
2	Cora Fabric Chair	10	2		
3	Tessa Fabric Chair	25	N/A		
4	Fabric Chair in a Box	9	2		
5	Lukah Leather Chair	10	2		
6	Fabric Tub Chair	4	1		
7	Fabric Wingback Chair	10	2		
8	Floral Fabric Tub Chair	15	3		
9	Habitat Oken Console Table	10	2		
10	Harley Fabric Cuddle Chair	10	2		
11	Leather Effect Tub Chair	5	1		
12	Habitat Fabric Chair	10	2		
13	Hygena Fabric Chair in a Box	5	1		
14	Hygena Lumina Console Table	15	3		

Formula explanation

=IFS(B2>20,"N/A",B2<=5,1, B2<=10,2, B2<20,3)

First, the formula has a test to mark the Reorder Priority of products greater than 20 as "N/A" (not applicable) as those have no re-order priority yet. Then several tests are defined in sequential order from the smallest value to the largest to ensure that the right corresponding value is returned as soon as a test is passed.

> **Tip** You can also apply **conditional formatting** to highlight the records with the highest priority. In this case, 1 is the highest priority. See my *Excel 2022 Basics* book for how to conditionally format a range.

SWITCH Function

The SWITCH function evaluates an expression against a list of values and returns the value corresponding to the first match. If no match is found, an optional default value may be returned. SWITCH allows you to identify values in your list and replace them with something more meaningful to your audience.

Syntax

=SWITCH(expression, value1, result1, [default or value2, result2],...[default or value3, result3])

Arguments

Argument	Description
expression	Required. The value that's compared against the list of values in value1 to value126. This argument can be a number, date, or text.
value1 to value126	Value1 is required. A value that will be compared with the expression argument. You can have up to 126 values.
result1 to result126	Result1 is required. The value that is returned when the corresponding argument matches the expression argument. A result must be supplied for each corresponding value argument. You can have up to 126 results to match each value argument.
default	Optional. The default value to return if no match is found. The argument must be the last one in the function. It is identified by not having a corresponding result value.

Remarks:

Excel functions are limited to 254 arguments, so you can only use up to 126 pairs of *value/result* arguments.

Example

The following example shows a column in our data representing the quarter. To make the data more understandable, we want to switch the numbers to text descriptions that describe the numbers more meaningfully.

List of values to switch:
- 1 = QTR1
- 2 = QTR2
- 3 = QTR3
- 4 = QTR4

Formula:

=SWITCH(C2,1,"QTR1",2,"QTR2",3,"QTR3",4,"QTR4","No match")

D2			*fx*	=SWITCH(C2,1,"QTR1",2,"QTR2",3,"QTR3",4,"QTR4","No match")					
	A	B	C	D	E	F	G	H	I
1	**Amount**	**Year**	**QTR**	**Switched**					
2	$1,242.00	2022	3	QTR3					
3	$3,221.00	2022	2	QTR2					
4	$2,349.00	2022	4	QTR4					
5	$2,951.00	2022	1	QTR1					
6	$1,903.00	2023	3	QTR3					
7	$2,648.80	2023	2	QTR2					
8	$2,754.00	2023	3	QTR3					
9	$2,859.20	2023	4	QTR4					
10	$2,964.40	2023	1	QTR1					
11									

A "No match" result would reveal an error in the data.

> **Tip** The *result* arguments have been entered directly in the formula here for demonstration purposes only. In a production worksheet, it would be better to enter the values in a lookup range in your worksheet and then use cell references in your formula. That way, it is easier to maintain.

AND Function

The AND function is used to determine if all conditions in a test are TRUE. This function is useful for scenarios where you want to perform more than one logical test and check that they all evaluate to TRUE before a condition is applied or calculated.

Syntax

=AND(logical1, [logical2], ...)

Arguments

Argument	Description
Logical1	Required. The first condition that you want to test that can either evaluate to TRUE or FALSE.
Logical2, ...	Optional. You can have up to 254 additional conditions you want to test that can evaluate to either TRUE or FALSE.

Remarks

- The arguments must evaluate to logical values (i.e., TRUE or FALSE) or must be references to cells that contain logical values.

- If an argument contains a reference that points to text values or empty cells, those values will be ignored.

- Excel returns the #VALUE! error if any referenced ranges contain no logical values.

Example

In this example, we want to apply a discount for order items that meet a certain criterion.

We want a formula that:

1. Checks that a product is on promotion.

2. Checks that the number of units ordered is three or more.

3. Applies a discount if the item is on promotion **and** three or more have been ordered.

	A	B	C
1	**Product Name**	**On Promotion**	**Units Ordered**
2	Chai	Yes	3
3	Syrup	Yes	1
4	Cajun Seasoning	Yes	6
5	Olive Oil	No	7
6	Boysenberry Spread	Yes	1
7	Dried Pears	No	1
8	Curry Sauce	Yes	2
9	Walnuts	Yes	3
10	Fruit Cocktail	No	4
11	Chocolate Biscuits Mix	Yes	2
12	Marmalade	Yes	3
13	Scones	Yes	5
14	Beer	Yes	10
15	Crab Meat	No	7

The AND formula we use to carry out both tests is:

AND(B2="yes",C2>=3)

Next, we use the AND function as an argument inside an IF function. The IF statement returns "Yes" if the AND statement returns TRUE and "No" if the AND statement returns FALSE.

The final formula looks like this:

=IF(AND(B2="yes",C2>=3)=TRUE,"Yes","No")

D2			fx	=IF(AND(B2="yes",C2>=3)=TRUE,"Yes","No")	

⊿	A	B	C	D	E
1	**Product Name**	**On Promotion**	**Units Ordered**	**Discount applied**	
2	Chai	Yes	3	Yes	
3	Syrup	Yes	1	No	
4	Cajun Seasoning	Yes	6	Yes	
5	Olive Oil	No	7	No	
6	Boysenberry Spread	Yes	1	No	
7	Dried Pears	No	1	No	
8	Curry Sauce	Yes	2	No	
9	Walnuts	Yes	3	Yes	
10	Fruit Cocktail	No	4	No	
11	Chocolate Biscuits Mix	Yes	2	No	
12	Marmalade	Yes	3	Yes	
13	Scones	Yes	5	Yes	
14	Beer	Yes	10	Yes	
15	Crab Meat	No	7	No	
16					

Our formula uses the AND function to extend the power of the IF function. Using AND as an argument in IF enabled us to perform two logical tests within its *logical_test* argument and return one logical value.

OR Function

The OR function is used to determine if any conditions in a test are TRUE. This function is useful for formulas where you want to perform more than one logical test and return a value if at least one of them evaluates to TRUE.

This function is best used in conjunction with other logical functions for more complex test scenarios involving multiple logical tests. For example, the IF function requires you to test a condition to determine which return statement to execute. If you combine IF and OR, it enables you to test multiple conditions instead of just one.

Syntax

=OR(logical1, [logical2], ...)

Arguments

Argument	Description
Logical1	Required. The first condition that you want to test that can either evaluate to TRUE or FALSE.
Logical2, ...	Optional. You can have up to 254 additional conditions you want to test that can evaluate to either TRUE or FALSE.

Remarks

- The maximum number of arguments you can have for the OR functions is 255.

- The arguments must evaluate to logical values (i.e., TRUE or FALSE) or must be references to cells that contain logical values.

- If an argument contains references that point to text or empty cells, those values will be ignored.

- If the specified range contains no logical values, Excel returns the #VALUE! error.

Example

In this example, we need to determine which sales staff qualify for a sales commission based on their generated sales.

The sales figures are in the table below. Under the main table, we have a lookup table for the Amount per **Criteria**. These are the goals referenced in our formula to calculate the **Commission** for each salesperson.

The IF function can be combined with OR to achieve our aim.

The following formula is entered in cell D2 and copied to the other cells in column D using the Fill Handle.

=IF(OR(B2>=$B$15,C2>=$B$16),B2*$B$17,0)

D2			fx	=IF(OR(B2>=$B$15,C2>=$B$16),B2*$B$17,0)	
	A	B	C	D	E
1	Name	Sales	Signups	Commission	Bonus
2	Nancy Freehafer	$12,500	20	$250	$188
3	Andrew Cencini	$14,300	25	$286	$215
4	Jan Kotas	$9,000	10	$180	$0
5	Mariya Sergienko	$8,050	5	$161	$0
6	Steven Thorpe	$5,000	7	$0	$0
7	Michael Neipper	$8,900	10	$178	$0
8	Robert Zare	$7,900	10	$0	$0
9	Laura Giussani	$6,000	17	$120	$0
10	Anne Hellung-Larsen	$11,000	18	$220	$0
11					
12				- Sales people need to exceed **Sales Goal**	
13				OR **Signup Goal** to earn a **Commission**.	
14	Criteria	Amount			
15	Sales Goal	$8,000		- Sales people need to exceed **Bonus Goal**	
16	Signup Goal	15		AND **Signup Goal** to earn a **Bonus**.	
17	Commission	2.0%			
18	Bonus Goal	$12,000			
19	Bonus %	1.5%			

Formula explanation

=IF(OR(B2>=$B$15,C2>=$B$16),B2*$B$17,0)

The formula says:

If the sales value is greater than or equal to the **Sales Goal**, OR signups are greater than or equal to the **Signup Goal**, then multiply Sales by the Commission (2.0%). Otherwise, return 0.

Trapping and Replacing Error Values

Excel provides formulas that enable you to catch error return values and replace them with a more user-friendly message. These functions are used with formulas where you anticipate error values in certain scenarios. Instead of displaying the error value on the worksheet, you can swap in a more meaningful message.

IFERROR Function

You can use IFERROR to trap errors in Excel formulas and return a custom message. This function provides a more user-friendly experience, especially if you're developing a worksheet for end-users and anticipate errors in certain data cells. Otherwise, you often do need to see the errors Excel generates so you can fix them.

This method is similar to how errors are trapped and handled in computer code. IFERROR can trap the following error types: #VALUE!, #N/A, #DIV/0!, #REF!, #NAME?, #NUM!, or #NULL!.

Syntax

=IFERROR(value, value_if_error)

Arguments

Argument	Description
value	Required. A cell reference or formula that's checked for an error.
value_if_error	Required. The value to be returned if the formula identifies an error.

Remarks

- If either *value* or *value_if_error* points to an empty cell, IFERROR treats it as an empty string value ("").

- If *value* is an array formula, IFERROR returns an array, one for each cell in the results range.

Example

In the following example, we use the IFERROR formula to trap any errors in our formula in column C and return a text message **Entry error**.

The FORMULATEXT function used in D2:D9 reveals the formulas in C2:C9.

C2			fx	=IFERROR(B2/A2,"Entry error")
	A	B	C	D
1	Target	Actual sold	Percentage	Formula text
2	200	35	18%	=IFERROR(B2/A2,"Entry error")
3	10	0	0%	=IFERROR(B3/A3,"Entry error")
4	120	50	42%	=IFERROR(B4/A4,"Entry error")
5	300	5	2%	=IFERROR(B5/A5,"Entry error")
6	0	60	Entry error	=IFERROR(B6/A6,"Entry error")
7	50	0	0%	=IFERROR(B7/A7,"Entry error")
8		10	Entry error	=IFERROR(B8/A8,"Entry error")
9	250	120	48%	=IFERROR(B9/A9,"Entry error")
10				

IFNA Function

The IFNA function is for handling #N/A errors. Excel displays the #NA error when a value is unavailable to a formula or function. Use IFNA when you want to trap and handle only #N/A errors.

You're more likely to encounter #N/A errors with lookup and reference functions when a value referenced in the formula is not in the source. You usually want to display other errors as they may reveal bugs in your formula that need fixing.

IFNA returns the value you specify if your formula encounters the #N/A error. Otherwise, it returns the result of the formula.

Syntax:

= IFNA(value, value_if_na)

Arguments

Argument	Description
value	Required. The expression that is checked for an error. It can be a value, cell reference, or formula. When using IFNA with VLOOKUP, the VLOOKUP formula will be this argument.
value_if_na	Required. The value the formula returns when it encounters a #N/A error.

Example

The following example uses the IFNA function to handle a #N/A error generated when the VLOOKUP function cannot find the provided lookup_value in the table_array.

The formula in E2, without IFNA, returns #N/A. Conversely, the formula in E3 traps the error with IFNA and provides a more user-friendly message.

=IFNA(VLOOKUP(D3,A3:B11,2,FALSE),"Not found")

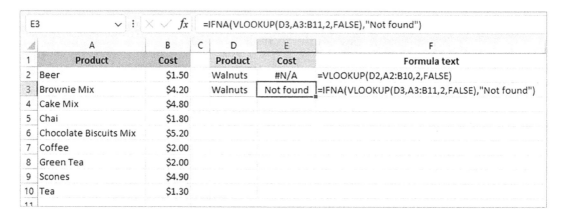

Chapter 4

Math Functions

This chapter covers functions that enable you to:

- Sum up data in contiguous or non-contiguous ranges.

- Sum up data based on certain criteria using a single function.

- Use multiple criteria to determine which data to add up.

- Generate random numbers between two given numbers.

- Generate a sequence of numbers based on given parameters.

- Automatically round up or round down numbers with a function.

- Calculate the square root of a number.

The mathematics functions in Excel can be found by clicking the Math & Trig command button on the Formulas tab of the ribbon. The dropdown menu lists all the Math & Trig functions. This category of functions in Excel ranges from common arithmetic functions to complex functions used by mathematicians and engineers.

Our focus here will be on the arithmetic functions, as many Excel trigonometric functions apply to math problems requiring specialist knowledge outside the scope of this book.

Summing and Aggregating Values

Excel offers an array of functions to sum values for different scenarios. You can create formulas that sum single ranges, multiple ranges, or values that meet certain criteria.

SUM Function

The SUM function enables you to sum up values on your spreadsheet. You can add individual values, cell references, ranges, or a mix of all three. You can sum up contiguous cells or non-contiguous cells.

Syntax

=SUM(number1,[number2],...)

Arguments

Argument	Description
Number1	Required. The first cell reference, range, or number for which you want to calculate the sum. The argument can be a number like 4, a cell reference like A10, or a range like A2:A10.
Number2, ...	Optional. Additional cell references, ranges, or numbers for which you want to calculate the sum - up to a maximum of 255.

Example 1

The following example sums up the values in cells B2 to B13. The SUM function was entered in the formula bar, but you can also use the AutoSum command on the ribbon to sum up the range.

=SUM(B2:B13)

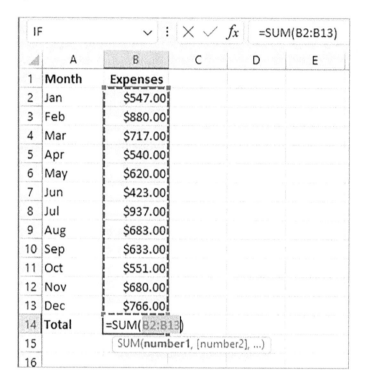

Example 2

To sum up data in different ranges, i.e., non-contiguous data, you can enter the ranges as different arguments in the SUM function.

=SUM(B2:B13,D2:D13,F2:F13,H2:H13)

	A	B	C	D	E	F	G	H	I
IF						=SUM(B2:B13,D2:D13,F2:F13,H2:H13)			
1	Month	Year1		Year2		Year3		Year4	
2	Jan	$547.00		$934.00		$412.00		$447.00	
3	Feb	$880.00		$590.00		$961.00		$605.00	
4	Mar	$717.00		$961.00		$460.00		$652.00	
5	Apr	$540.00		$542.00		$574.00		$754.00	
6	May	$620.00		$497.00		$531.00		$462.00	
7	Jun	$423.00		$874.00		$799.00		$699.00	
8	Jul	$937.00		$755.00		$877.00		$446.00	
9	Aug	$683.00		$715.00		$792.00		$742.00	
10	Sep	$633.00		$421.00		$877.00		$576.00	
11	Oct	$551.00		$941.00		$675.00		$598.00	
12	Nov	$680.00		$520.00		$867.00		$916.00	
13	Dec	$766.00		$524.00		$401.00		$707.00	
14									
15	Total							H13)	
16									

SUMIF Function

The SUMIF function combines a math function and a logical function. It allows you to sum up data in a range based on the specified criteria.

Syntax

=SUMIF(range, criteria, [sum_range])

Arguments

Argument	Description
range	Required. The range you want to evaluate based on the condition in *criteria*.
criteria	Required. The condition (or logical test) that is used to determine which cells are summed up in range. This value can be an expression, cell reference, text, or function.
	If this argument is text or includes logical or math symbols like greater than (>), it must be enclosed in double quotes (""). If criteria is numeric, quotation marks are not required.
sum_range	Optional. Used to specify the sum range if it is different from the range specified in the range. If omitted, the range argument is used.

Remarks

- Cells in the range argument must be numbers, names (for example, named ranges or tables), arrays, or references that contain numbers. Text values and blanks are ignored.

- You can use wildcard characters (like a question mark "?" or an asterisk "*") as the criteria argument. A question mark matches any single character, while an asterisk matches any sequence of characters. Type a tilde (~) before the character if you want to find an actual question mark or asterisk.

Example

The following example uses SUMIF to calculate the following:

- Total of all sales over $5,000.

- Total commissions paid out to salespeople who generated over $5,000 in sales.

We can achieve the desired results with two formulas:

=SUMIF(B2:B11,">5000")

=SUMIF(B2:B11,">5000", C2:C11)

	F2			f_x	=SUMIF(B2:B11,">5000")	
	A	B	C	D	E	F	G
1	Salesperson	Sales	Commission		Sales over $5K		Formula text
2	Geraldine Simpson	$2,635	$132		Total	$59,250	=SUMIF(B2:B11,">5000")
3	Earnest Lambert	$7,227	$361		Total comm.	$2,963	=SUMIF(B2:B11,">5000", C2:C11)
4	Pauline Turner	$4,426	$221				
5	Miriam Abbott	$4,774	$239				
6	Willis Goodwin	$9,829	$491				
7	Claire Wilkerson	$20,000	$1,000				
8	Jamie Newman	$2,459	$123				
9	Andres Craig	$11,300	$565				
10	Dominic Gilbert	$2,566	$128				
11	Luz Fitzgerald	$10,894	$545				

Formula explanation

=SUMIF(B2:B11,">5000")

This formula uses the criteria argument of ">5000" to filter which values will be added to the sum from the range B2:B11.

=SUMIF(B2:B11,">5000", C2:C11)

Our second formula uses the criteria argument ">5000" to select the values in range B2:B11 (Sales) for which the corresponding values in range C2:C11 (Commission) will be added to the sum. So, even though we applied the criteria to B2:B11, the calculated values returned by the formula come from C2:C11.

SUMIFS Function

The SUMIFS function is like the SUMIF function, but you can use multiple criteria to determine which cells in a range are included in the sum. SUMIFS enables you to have up to 127 range/criteria pairs.

Syntax

=SUMIFS(sum_range, criteria_range1, criteria1, [criteria_range2, criteria2], ...)

Arguments

Argument	Description
sum_range	Required. The range of cells to sum up.
criteria_range1	Required. The range that is tested using Criteria1.
	Criteria_range1 and criteria1 are a pair where criteria1 is used to search criteria_range1 for matching values. Once items in the range are found, Excel sums up their corresponding values in sum_range.
criteria1	Required. The criteria used to filter criteria_range1 to select a subset of data. For example, criteria can be entered as 40, ">40", C6, "bolts", or "125".
criteria_range2, criteria2, ...	Optional. You can have additional range/criteria pairs up to 127.

Remarks

- If you are testing for text values, ensure the criteria are in quotation marks.

- You can use wildcard characters like the question mark (?) and asterisk (*) in your criteria to enable you to find matches that are not exact but similar. The question mark matches one character, and the asterisk matches a sequence of characters. To find a character like a question mark or asterisk, type a tilde sign (~) in front of the character.

- The criteria_range argument must reference a range with the same number of rows and columns as the sum_range argument.

Example

The following example sums up sales data using two criteria:

1. State name.

2. Items with 40 or more Orders (>=40).

The following formula achieves the result:

=SUMIFS($D$2:$D$12,$B$2:$B$12,F2,$C$2:$C$12,G2)

H2				fx	=SUMIFS($D$2:$D$12,$B$2:$B$12,F2,$C$2:$C$12,G2)		
	A	B	C	D	E	F	G	H
1	Name	States	No. Orders	Sales		States	Orders	Total Sales for matching orders
2	Bruce	New York	51	$74,298		New York	>=40	$140,407
3	Louis	New York	39	$46,039		Texas	>=40	$44,390
4	Earl	Washington	60	$65,252		California	>=40	$42,484
5	Sean	Washington	100	$61,847		Washington	>=40	$127,099
6	Benjamin	Texas	28	$33,340				
7	Joe	California	31	$95,778				
8	Shawn	Texas	35	$58,808				
9	Kenneth	California	39	$52,593				
10	Cynthia	California	51	$42,484				
11	Susan	Texas	80	$44,390				
12	Dav	New York	70	$66,109				
13								

Formula explanation

=SUMIFS($D$2:$D$12,$B$2:$B$12,F2,$C$2:$C$12,G2)

- The sum_range argument references the Sales column **D2:D12** (an absolute reference has been used - **$D$2:$D$12**).

- The criteria_range1 is **B2:B12** (an absolute reference has also been used here - **$B$2:$B$12**).

- Press F4, with the argument selected, to make this an absolute reference.

- The criteria1 argument is **F2**, which is a reference to the states we want to use as our criteria. Using a cell reference makes it easier to change this value.

This argument has a relative reference because we want the cell reference to change as we copy the formula to other cells.

- The criteria_range2 is **$C$2:$C$12** (in absolute reference form).

- The criteria2 argument is **G2** (>=40). A cell reference has been used for this argument to make it easier to change.

We enter the formula in cell **H2** and then copy it down the column to calculate the **Total Sales** for orders that match the criteria for each state.

> **⟡Tip** To convert a relative reference to an absolute reference, manually add the dollar signs in the formula bar or select the reference in the formula (i.e., D2:D12) and press the **F4** key. Making the references absolute ensures they don't change when the formula is copied to other cells.

Using Named Ranges

One way to make a formula with absolute references easier to read is to use named ranges. Name ranges are absolute references by default and provide a cleaner look to your formula.

For example:
- Sales = D2:D12
- States = B2:B12
- Orders = C2:C12

With the named ranges in place, the formula looks like this:

=SUMIFS(Sales,States,F2,Orders,G2)

Instead of this:

=SUMIFS($D$2:$D$12,$B$2:$B$12,F2,$C$2:$C$12,G2)

IF			✓ : ✕ ✓ fx	=SUMIFS(Sales,States,F2,Orders,G2)			
	A	B	C		SUMIFS(sum_range, criteria_range1, criteria1, [criteria_range2, c		

	Name	States	No. Orders	Sales	States	Orders	Total Sales for matching orders
1	Name	States	No. Orders	Sales	States	Orders	
2	Bruce	New York	51	$74,298	New York	>=40	Orders,G2)
3	Louis	New York	39	$46,039	Texas	>=40	$44,390
4	Earl	Washington	60	$65,252	California	>=40	$42,484
5	Sean	Washington	100	$61,847	Washington	>=40	$127,099
6	Benjamin	Texas	28	$33,340			
7	Joe	California	31	$95,778			
8	Shawn	Texas	35	$58,808			
9	Kenneth	California	39	$52,593			
10	Cynthia	California	51	$42,484			
11	Susan	Texas	80	$44,390			
12	Dav	New York	70	$66,109			
13							

AGGREGATE Function

The AGGREGATE function returns an aggregate in a list or database. This function brings together all the aggregate functions into one. Instead of using individual aggregate functions, like SUM, AVG, MAX, etc., you simply enter a number in one of its arguments to specify the type of aggregate you want to perform. You can also set the option to ignore hidden rows and error values. You can perform 19 aggregate operations with this function.

There are two forms of the AGGREGATE function:

- Reference form
- Array form

Syntax

Reference form

=AGGREGATE(function_num, options, ref1, [ref2], ...)

Array form

=AGGREGATE(function_num, options, array, [k])

Arguments

- **Function_num:** Required. The function_num argument is a number between 1 and 19. This argument is the number that specifies which aggregate function to use. See the list below.

Function_num	Function
1	AVERAGE
2	COUNT
3	COUNTA
4	MAX
5	MIN
6	PRODUCT
7	STDEV.S
8	STDEV.P
9	SUM
10	VAR.S
11	VAR.P
12	MEDIAN
13	MODE.SNGL
14	LARGE
15	SMALL
16	PERCENTILE.INC
17	QUARTILE.INC
18	PERCENTILE.EXC
19	QUARTILE.EXC

- **Options:** Required. This argument is a numerical value from 1 to 7 that determines which values to ignore in the range evaluated.

Option	Behavior
0 or omitted	Ignore nested AGGREGATE and SUBTOTAL functions
1	Ignore hidden rows, nested AGGREGATE and SUBTOTAL functions
2	Ignore error values, nested AGGREGATE and SUBTOTAL functions
3	Ignore hidden rows, error values, nested AGGREGATE and SUBTOTAL functions
4	Ignore nothing
5	Ignore hidden rows
6	Ignore error values
7	Ignore hidden rows and error values

- **Ref1:** Required. The first argument for functions that take multiple numeric arguments. Ref1 can be a range, an array (for functions that take an array), or a formula.

- **Ref2**: Optional. For additional numeric arguments. You can have up to 253 arguments in total for which you want the aggregate value.

For the functions that take an array argument, ref1 will be an array, an array formula, or a reference to a range for which you want the aggregate. Ref2 is a second argument that is required for some functions. The functions listed below require a ref2 argument:

Function
LARGE(array,k)
SMALL(array,k)
PERCENTILE.INC(array,k)
QUARTILE.INC(array,quart)
PERCENTILE.EXC(array,k)
QUARTILE.EXC(array,quart)

Remarks

- As soon as you type **=AGGREGATE(** in the formula bar, you'll see a dropdown list of all functions that you can use as arguments for function_num. You'll also get a dropdown list of the values you can enter for the options argument.

- AGGREGATE will return a #VALUE! error if a second ref argument is required but not provided.

- The AGGREGATE function is designed for columns of data, i.e., vertical ranges. It is not designed for rows of data, i.e., horizontal ranges.

Examples

In the following example, we'll use different instances of the AGGREGATE function to evaluate the data in range A2:B12. The calculations use different function_num arguments for the AGGREGATE function.

	A	B	C	D	E	F
1	Table of numbers			Calculation	Result	Formula text
2	#DIV/0!	56		MAX (4)	150	=AGGREGATE(4, 6, A2:A12)
3	90	81		LARGE (14)	95	=AGGREGATE(14, 6, A2:B12, 3)
4	31	95		SMALL (15)	#VALUE!	=AGGREGATE(15, 6, A2:A12)
5	#NUM!	49		MEDIAN (12)	77.5	=AGGREGATE(12, 6, A2:A12, B2:B12)
6	41	34		MAX function	#DIV/0!	=MAX(A2:B12)
7	150	92				
8	34	58				
9	87	93				
10	33	120				
11	53	89				
12	74	92				
13						

Formulas and descriptions

Example 1 - MAX

Formula =AGGREGATE(4, 6, A2:B12)

Result 150

Description Returns the maximum value in range A2:B12 while ignoring error values.

Example 2 - LARGE

Formula =AGGREGATE(14, 6, A2:B12, 3)

Result 95

Description Returns the third largest value in range A2:B12 while ignoring error values.

Example 3 - SMALL

Formula	=AGGREGATE(15, 6, A2:B12)
Result	#VALUE!
Description	Returns a #VALUE! error because AGGREGATE is expecting a second ref argument here. The function referenced (SMALL) requires one.

Example 4 - MEDIAN

Formula	=AGGREGATE(12, 6, A2:A12, B2:B12)
Result	77.5
Description	Returns the median from both columns while ignoring error values in the range.

Example 5

Formula	=MAX(A2:B12)
Result	#DIV/0!
Description	The regular MAX function is used here for comparisons. It returns an error value since error values are in the referenced range.

> **Tip** The AGGREGATE function would be overkill for common aggregate calculations in Excel, like sum, average, and count. Hence, use standard functions like SUM, AVG, MIN, and MAX for common aggregate calculations. Only use AGGREGATE if you're calculating one of the more complex aggregate types like STDEV.S, QUARTILE.INC, PERCENTILE.INC etc.

Generating Random and Sequential Numbers

The functions in this category enable you to generate a series of random or sequential numbers between a given start and end number, including an interval if required.

RANDBETWEEN Function

The RANDBETWEEN function returns a random integer between two numbers you specify. This function comes in handy whenever you need to generate sample data between two numbers. For example, if you want to generate sample data between 1 and 100 in several cells, you could use RANDBETWEEN to generate a random number in one cell and copy the formula over the required range.

Syntax

=RANDBETWEEN(bottom, top)

Arguments

Argument	Description
Bottom	Required. The smallest integer to be returned.
Top	Required. The largest integer to be returned.

Random values from RANDBETWEEN are regenerated each time the worksheet is recalculated. If you don't want the values to change each time the worksheet is recalculated, copy them to the clipboard, then use **Paste Special** > **Values** to convert them to static values.

To generate a random number that doesn't change, enter the formula in the formula bar, press F9 to convert the formula to a static value, then press **Enter** to insert the value in the cell.

Example

The following example uses RANDBETWEEN to generate sample data for student scores between 0 and 100.

= RANDBETWEEN(0,100)

B4				fx	=RANDBETWEEN(0,100)	
	A	B	C	D	E	F
1	**Test Score Sample Data**					
2						
3	**Student**	Score				
4	Bruce	70				
5	Louis	82				
6	Earl	28				
7	Sean	44				
8	Benjamin	3				
9	Joe	19				
10	Shawn	38				
11	Kenneth	34				
12	Cynthia	5				
13	Susan	7				

Tip To keep only the generated values without the formula, generate the sample data in a different part of your worksheet and copy and paste only the values into your target range. For example, if you wanted random values in cells B2:B10, generate the values using RANDBETWEEN in cells C2:C10 and then copy and paste only the values in B2:B10, then delete the values in C2:C10.

RANDARRAY Function

RANDARRAY is a dynamic array function that returns random numbers. An array can be seen as a row of values, a column of values, or a combination of both. This function is an improvement on RANDBETWEEN, which returns only one value and must be copied to the entire range for multiple random numbers. RANDARRAY can return multiple values with one formula for your specified range. You can also specify whether you want whole numbers or decimal values.

 Note This function is currently only available to Microsoft 365 subscribers.

Syntax

=RANDARRAY([rows],[columns],[min],[max],[whole_number])

Argument	Description
rows	Optional. The number of rows returned. If omitted, RANDARRAY will return a single row.
columns	Optional. The number of columns returned. If omitted, RANDARRAY will return a single column.
min	Optional. The minimum number to return.
max	Optional. The maximum number to return.
whole_number	Optional. Set this option to TRUE for whole numbers and FALSE for decimal values.
	If omitted, the default is FALSE, i.e., decimal values.

Remarks:

- If you omit both the rows and columns arguments, RANDARRAY returns a single value.

- If you omit the min and max arguments, RANDARRY returns numbers between 0 and 1.

- The max argument must be greater than the min argument. Otherwise, RANDARRAY returns a #VALUE! error.

Example

The following example generates sample numbers to be used as test data. The RANDARRAY formula is in cell B2, spilling the result over the range B2:E13. Note that we do not need to copy the formula to the other cells.

=RANDARRAY(12,4,500,1000,TRUE)

	A	B	C	D	E	F	G
1		2022	2023	2024	2025		
2	Jan	$501.00	$817.00	$530.00	$711.00		
3	Feb	$959.00	$887.00	$710.00	$739.00		
4	Mar	$532.00	$794.00	$727.00	$894.00		
5	Apr	$668.00	$972.00	$759.00	$839.00		
6	May	$945.00	$683.00	$751.00	$698.00		
7	Jun	$978.00	$509.00	$561.00	$911.00		
8	Jul	$626.00	$669.00	$911.00	$915.00		
9	Aug	$662.00	$573.00	$849.00	$971.00		
10	Sep	$829.00	$699.00	$966.00	$962.00		
11	Oct	$822.00	$813.00	$719.00	$720.00		
12	Nov	$751.00	$823.00	$889.00	$998.00		
13	Dec	$692.00	$983.00	$878.00	$884.00		
14							

Cell reference B2 with formula: =RANDARRAY(12,4,500,1000,TRUE)

Formula explanation

=RANDARRAY(12,4,500,1000,TRUE)

The row and column numbers are 12 and 4. The min and max numbers are 500 and 1000. The whole_number argument is set to TRUE to return whole numbers. The range is formatted as Currency.

> **Note** Random values from RANDARRAY are regenerated each time the worksheet is recalculated. If you don't want the values to change each time the worksheet is recalculated, copy them to the clipboard, then use **Paste Special** > **Values** to convert them to static values.

SEQUENCE Function

SEQUENCE is a dynamic array function that allows you to generate a list of sequential numbers in an array. You can also specify an interval. An array can be a row of values, a column of values, or a combination of both. You can manually generate a series of numbers in Excel using the AutoFill feature. SEQUENCE offers the function equivalent of creating a series.

 Note This function is currently only available to Microsoft 365 subscribers.

Syntax

=SEQUENCE(rows,[columns],[start],[step])

Arguments

Argument	Description
rows	Required. The number of rows to create.
columns	Optional. The number of columns to create. The default is 1 if this argument is omitted.
start	Optional. The starting number. The default is 1 if this argument is omitted.
step	Optional. The increment applied to each subsequent value in the array. The default is 1 if this argument is omitted.

Remarks

The result from SEQUENCE will spill on the worksheet if it's the final result of a formula. Excel will create the right-sized range to display the result. You can also use SEQUENCE as an argument within another formula to generate an array of values.

Example 1

The following example uses SEQUENCE to generate even numbers in five columns and five rows.

=SEQUENCE(5,5,0,2)

The formula has 5 for both the rows and columns arguments. The start argument is 0, and the step is 2.

	A	B	C	D	E	F
			fx	=SEQUENCE(5,5,0,2)		
1	0	2	4	6	8	
2	10	12	14	16	18	
3	20	22	24	26	28	
4	30	32	34	36	38	
5	40	42	44	46	48	
6						
7						
8						

Example 2

Excel stores date values internally as serial numbers, so you can use SEQUENCE to generate dates with a specified interval. To display the result as a date, ensure the spill range is formatted as an Excel **Date**.

The following example generates the Monday date for 10 weeks from our specified starting date, 10/10/2022.

	B2				f_x	=SEQUENCE(10,,DATEVALUE("10/10/2022"),7)				
	A	B	C	D	E	F	G	H
1	Week starting Monday							
2	Week 1	10/10/2022						
3	Week 2	17/10/2022						
4	Week 3	24/10/2022						
5	Week 4	31/10/2022						
6	Week 5	07/11/2022						
7	Week 6	14/11/2022						
8	Week 7	21/11/2022						
9	Week 8	28/11/2022						
10	Week 9	05/12/2022						
11	Week 10	12/12/2022						
12								

Formula explanation:

=SEQUENCE(10,,DATEVALUE("10/10/2022"),7)

The rows argument is 10 to specify the ten rows of dates we want to return. The columns argument has been omitted as we only want one column. For the starting date, the formula uses the DATEVALUE function to return the serial number for the provided date string. The step argument is 7, which increments each subsequent number by 7. Excel displays the serial numbers returned by DATEVALUE as dates because the spill range has the Date number format.

> **Note** You might be thinking that it would just be easier to generate the list of dates on the worksheet by adding 7 to the second week and using autofill to populate the other cells. That's correct. The SEQUENCE function is more useful when you need to generate sequential values as an array argument within another formula.

Rounding Numbers

The functions in this category enable you to create formulas that round numbers up or down in different ways, based on the settings you provide.

ROUND Function

The ROUND function rounds a number to a specified number of digits. For example, if you have 25.4568 in cell A1 and you want to round the figure to two decimal places, you can use the following formula:

=ROUND(A1, 2)

The function will return: 25.46

Syntax

=ROUND(number, num_digits)

Arguments

Argument	Description
number	Required. This argument is the number that you want to round.
num_digits	Required. The number of decimal places to which you want to round the number.

Remarks

- The number is rounded to the specified number of decimal places if num_digits is greater than 0 (zero).
- The number is rounded to the nearest integer if num_digits is 0.
- The number is rounded to the left of the decimal point if num_digits is less than 0.
- Use the ROUNDUP function to always round up (away from zero).
- Use the ROUNDDOWN function to always round down (toward zero).

Examples

In the following examples, the ROUND function is applied to several values. The table displays the formula, the result, and a description of the outcome.

Formula	Result	Description
=ROUND(3.15, 1)	3.2	Rounds 3.15 to one decimal place.
=ROUND(4.149, 1)	4.1	Rounds 4.149 to one decimal place.
=ROUND(-2.475, 2)	-2.48	Rounds -2.475 to two decimal places.
=ROUND(57.5, -1)	60	Rounds 57.5 to one decimal place to the left of the decimal point.
=ROUND(671.3,-3)	1000	Rounds 671.3 to the nearest multiple of 1000.
=ROUND(1.78,-1)	0	Rounds 1.78 to the nearest multiple of 10.
=ROUND(-70.45,-2)	-100	Rounds -70.45 to the nearest multiple of 100.

ROUNDUP Function

The ROUNDUP function rounds a number up, away from 0 (zero).

Syntax

=ROUNDUP(number, num_digits)

Arguments

Argument	Description
number	Required. This argument is for the number that you want to round up.
num_digits	Required. The number of decimal places to which you want to round up the number.

Remarks

- ROUNDUP is like ROUND but always rounds a number up.
- Number is rounded up to the specified number of decimal places if num_digits is greater than 0 (zero).
- Number is rounded up to the nearest integer if num_digits is 0.
- Number is rounded up to the left of the decimal point if num_digits is less than 0.

Examples

In the following examples, ROUNDUP is applied to several values. The table displays the value, result, formula, and description.

	A	B	C	D
1	Value	Rounded up	Formula text	Description
2	3.15	3.2	=ROUNDUP(A2, 1)	Rounds 3.15 up to one decimal place.
3	4.149	5	=ROUNDUP(A3, 0)	Rounds 4.149 up to zero decimal places.
4	-2.475	-2.48	=ROUNDUP(A4, 2)	Rounds -2.475 to two decimal places.
5	57.5	60	=ROUNDUP(A5, -1)	Rounds 57.5 to one decimal place to the left of the decimal point.
6	671.3	700	=ROUNDUP(A6,-2)	Rounds 671.3 to two decimal places to the left of the decimal point.
7	1.78	2	=ROUNDUP(A7,0)	Rounds 1.78 up to zero decimal places.
8	-70.45	-100	=ROUNDUP(A8,-2)	Rounds -70.45 to the nearest multiple of 100.
9				
10				
11				
12				
13				

Formula explanations

=ROUNDUP(A2, 1)

In the formula above, A2 is the cell reference to the value to be rounded up. The num_digits argument is 1, specifying that we want to round up to 1 decimal place.

=ROUNDUP(A3, 0)

In the formula above, A3 is the cell reference to the value to round up. The num_digits argument is 0, specifying that we want to round up to a whole number, i.e., zero decimal places.

=ROUNDUP(A5, -1)

In the formula above, the num_digits argument is -1, specifying that we want to round up to one decimal place to the left of the decimal point. So, 57.5 is rounded up to 60.

ROUNDDOWN Function

The ROUNDDOWN function rounds a number down towards zero.

Syntax

=ROUNDDOWN(number, num_digits)

Arguments

Argument	Description
number	Required. The number you want to round down.
num_digits	Required. The number of decimal places you want to round the number down to.

Remarks

- ROUNDDOWN works like ROUND but always rounds a number down.

- Number is rounded down to the specified number of decimal places if num_digits is greater than 0 (zero).

- Number is rounded down to the nearest integer if num_digits is 0.

- Number is rounded down to the left of the decimal point if num_digits is less than 0.

Examples

In the following examples, ROUNDDOWN is applied to several values. The table displays the value, result, formula, and description.

	A	B	C	D
1	Value	Result	Formula text	Description
2	3.15	3.1	=ROUNDDOWN(A2, 1)	Rounds 3.15 down to one decimal place.
3	4.149	4	=ROUNDDOWN(A3, 0)	Rounds 4.149 down to zero decimal places.
4	-2.475	-2.47	=ROUNDDOWN(A4, 2)	Rounds -2.475 down to two decimal places.
5	57.5	50	=ROUNDDOWN(A5, -1)	Rounds 57.5 down to one decimal place to the left of the decimal point.
6	671.3	600	=ROUNDDOWN(A6,-2)	Rounds 671.3 down to the nearest multiple of 100.
7	1.78	1	=ROUNDDOWN(A7,0)	Rounds 1.78 down to zero decimal places.
8	-71.45	-70	=ROUNDDOWN(A8,-1)	Rounds -71.45 down to the nearest multiple of 10.
9				

Formula explanations

= ROUNDDOWN(A2, 1)

In the formula above, A2 is the cell reference holding the value to be rounded down. The num_digits argument is 1, specifying that we want to round down to 1 decimal place. So, 3.15 is rounded down to 3.1.

= ROUNDDOWN(A3, 0)

In the formula above, A3 is the cell reference to the value to round down. The num_digits argument is 0, specifying that we want to round down to a whole number, i.e., zero decimal places. So, 4.149 is rounded down to 4.

=ROUNDDOWN(A5, -1)

In the formula above, A5 is the cell reference to the value to round down. The num_digits argument is -1, specifying that we want to round down to one decimal place to the left of the decimal point. So, 57.5 is rounded down to 50.

Other Math Functions

The functions in this section are useful for performing calculations that return values as arguments within other functions.

Returning the Reminder with MOD

The MOD function is useful for calculations where you want to return the remainder of a division between two numbers. The result has the same sign as the divisor.

Syntax

=MOD(number, divisor)

Arguments

Argument	Description
Number	Required. The number being divided for which you want to find the remainder.
Divisor	Required. The number being used for the division. MOD will return the #DIV/0! error value if the divisor is 0.

Examples

The following examples use MOD in column C to calculate the remainder by dividing the values in column A by the values in column B.

C2			f_x	=MOD(A2,B2)

	A	B	C	D
1	**Number**	**Divisor**	**Result**	**Description**
2	100	40	20	Reminder of 100/40
3	7	5	2	Reminder of 7/5
4	30	45	30	
5	-4	3	2	The result is always the same sign as the divisor.
6	-3	2	1	
7	4	-3	-2	Result is always the same sign as the divisor.
8	-4	-3	-1	
9				

Returning The Square Root with SQRT

This function returns a positive square root of any number.

Syntax

=SQRT(number)

Argument	Description
number	Required. The number for which you want to calculate the square root.
	The function returns an error value (#NUM!) if this value is negative.

Example

The SQRT function has been applied to the following numbers.

| B2 | | ⌄ ⋮ ✕ ✓ | fx | =SQRT(A2) |

◢	A	B	C
1	**Number**	**Square root**	
2	16	4	
3	6602	81.25269226	
4	4414	66.43794097	
5	5788	76.07890641	
6	1216	34.87119155	
7	0	0	
8	1	1	
9	820	28.63564213	
10	852	29.18903904	
11	6358	79.73706792	
12	924	30.39736831	
13	8689	93.21480569	
14	6614	81.32650245	
15	-10	#NUM!	Negative numner
16	4163	64.52131431	
17	8942	94.56214888	
18	2628	51.26402247	
19	4010	63.3245608	
20	9465	97.28823156	
21			

Chapter 5

Statistical Functions

This chapter covers functions that enable you to:

- Calculate the average, min, max, and median values in a range.

- Use criteria to determine which values to aggregate.

- Count the number of values in a range of cells that meet a certain condition.

- Count the number of values in a range that meet multiple criteria.

- Count the number of cells that contain numbers in a range or table.

- Count the number of empty cells in a range or table.

You can access the statistical functions in Excel by clicking on the More Functions button on the Formulas tab. On the drop-down menu, highlight the Statistical option to display a list of all the statistical functions in alphabetical order. The statistical functions in Excel range from everyday statistical functions like AVERAGE, MIN, MAX, etc., to more specialized functions used by statisticians.

Counting Values

Excel provides an array of functions that enable you to count values in your worksheet. You can count all populated cells, only numeric values, blank values, or values that meet certain criteria.

COUNT Function

The COUNT function will count the number of cells that contain numbers in a range or a list of numbers provided as arguments. The COUNT function only counts populated cells. For example, if you have a range with 20 cells, and only 5 cells have numbers, the count function will return 5.

Syntax

=COUNT(value1, [value2], ...)

Arguments

Argument	Description
Value1	Required. The first range in which you want to count numbers.
Value2	Optional. Additional cell references or ranges in which you want to count numbers. You can have a maximum of 255 arguments for this function.

Remarks

- You can have a maximum of 255 arguments for this function. Each argument could be a number, a cell reference, or a range.

- The COUNT function counts numbers, dates, or text representations of numbers (i.e., a number enclosed in quotation marks, like "1").

- Error values or text that cannot be translated into numbers are not counted.

- Use the COUNTA function if you want to count text, logical values, or error values.

- Use the COUNTIF function or the COUNTIFS function to count only numbers that meet a specific condition.

Example

The following formula counts the values in two ranges:

=COUNT(A3:D20,F3:I20)

This formula has two arguments to represent the ranges in which we want to count values: A3:D20 and F3:I20. Note that the blank cells are not counted.

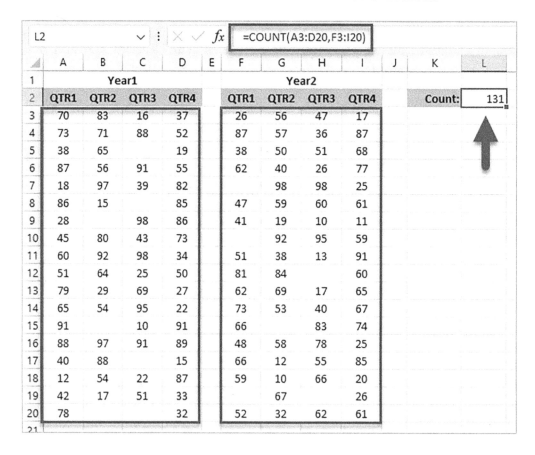

L2						fx	=COUNT(A3:D20,F3:I20)					
	A	B	C	D	E	F	G	H	I	J	K	L
1		Year1					Year2					
2	QTR1	QTR2	QTR3	QTR4		QTR1	QTR2	QTR3	QTR4		Count:	131
3	70	83	16	37		26	56	47	17			
4	73	71	88	52		87	57	36	87			
5	38	65		19		38	50	51	68			
6	87	56	91	55		62	40	26	77			
7	18	97	39	82			98	98	25			
8	86	15		85		47	59	60	61			
9	28		98	86		41	19	10	11			
10	45	80	43	73			92	95	59			
11	60	92	98	34		51	38	13	91			
12	51	64	25	50		81	84		60			
13	79	29	69	27		62	69	17	65			
14	65	54	95	22		73	53	40	67			
15	91		10	91		66		83	74			
16	88	97	91	89		48	58	78	25			
17	40	88		15		66	12	55	85			
18	12	54	22	87		59	10	66	20			
19	42	17	51	33			67		26			
20	78			32		52	32	62	61			
21												

COUNTIF Function

The COUNTIF function is a combination of a statistical function and a logical function. It allows you to count the number of cells that meet a criterion. For example, you can count only the values in a list of orders that exceed $1,000.

Syntax

=COUNTIF(range, criteria)

Arguments

Argument	Description
range	Required. The group of cells that you want to count. This argument can contain numbers, a named range, or references that contain numbers.
criteria	Required. The condition used to determine which cells will be counted. This argument can be a cell reference, text, expression, or function. For example, you can use a number like 40, a logical comparison like ">=40", a cell reference like D10, or a word like "bolts."

Remarks

- If the criteria argument is a text value or includes logical or math symbols, like greater than (>), it must be enclosed in double quotes ("").

- If criteria is a numeric value, quotation marks are not required.

Example

In this example, we're using COUNTIF to count all Sales over $5,000.

The formula we use is:

=COUNTIF(B2:B11,">5000")

C14				f_x	=COUNTIF(B2:B11,">5000")	
	A	B	C		D	
1	Salesperson	Sales	Commission		Formula text	
2	Bruce	$2,635	$132			
3	Louis	$7,227	$361			
4	Earl	$4,426	$221			
5	Sean	$4,774	$239			
6	Benjamin	$9,829	$491			
7	Joe	$20,000	$1,000			
8	Shawn	$2,459	$123			
9	Kenneth	$11,300	$565			
10	Cynthia	$2,566	$128			
11	Susan	$10,894	$545			
12						
13	Report					
14	Count of sales over $5,000		5	=COUNTIF(B2:B11,">5000")		
15	Count of commissions over $200		7	=COUNTIF(C2:C11,">200")		
16						

The first argument is the range we want to count - **B2:B11**.

The second argument is the criteria - greater than $5,000 (">5000").

Note that the criteria argument is enclosed in quotes because it includes a comparison operator.

Other examples

In the following examples, we have a list of orders that we query with different COUNTIF formulas in a report. The results and formulas are shown in the image below.

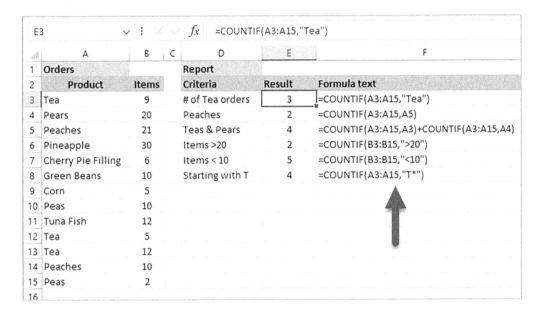

COUNTIFS Function

The COUNTIFS function enables you to count values in multiple ranges using multiple criteria to determine the values to count.

Syntax

=COUNTIFS(criteria_range1, criteria1, [criteria_range2, criteria2]…)

Arguments

Argument	Description
criteria_range1	Required. The first range you want to evaluate using the associated criteria, which is criteria1.
criteria1	Required. The first criteria argument, which pairs with criteria_range1. It could be a number, cell reference, expression, or text that defines which cells will be counted. For example, criteria can be expressed as 40, ">=40", D10, "bolts", or "40".
criteria_range2, criteria2, ...	Optional. Additional ranges and criteria pairs. You can have a total of 127 range/criteria pairs.

Remarks

- Each additional range must have the same number of rows and columns as criteria_range1. The ranges do not have to be adjacent to each other.

- If the criteria argument points to an empty cell, the COUNTIFS function treats the empty cell as a 0 value.

- If you are testing for text values, for example, "apples," make sure the criterion is in quotation marks.

- You can use wildcard characters like the question mark (?) and asterisk (*) in your criteria to enable you to find matches that are similar but not the same. The question mark matches any character, and the asterisk matches a sequence of characters. To find a character like a question mark or asterisk, type a tilde sign (~) in front of the character.

Example

The following example counts the number of people for each State with 40 or more Orders. This problem requires using two criteria to evaluate two columns. We will use the state name and ">=40" to filter the rows to be counted.

We apply the following formula to solve the problem:

=COUNTIFS(State,F2,Orders,G2)

Range names:
- State = B2:B12
- Orders = C2:C12

	A	B	C	D	E	F	G	H	I
1	Name	State	Orders	Sales		States	Orders	# People	Formula text
2	Bruce	New York	51	$74,298		New York	>=40	2	=COUNTIFS(State,F2,Orders,G2)
3	Louis	New York	39	$46,039		Texas	>=40	1	=COUNTIFS(State,F3,Orders,G3)
4	Earl	Washington	60	$65,252		California	>=40	1	=COUNTIFS(State,F4,Orders,G4)
5	Sean	Washington	100	$61,847		Washington	>=40	2	=COUNTIFS(State,F5,Orders,G5)
6	Benjamin	Texas	28	$33,340					
7	Joe	California	31	$95,778					
8	Shawn	Texas	35	$58,808					
9	Kenneth	California	39	$52,593					
10	Cynthia	California	51	$42,484		State = B2:B12			
11	Susan	Texas	80	$44,390		Orders = C2:12			
12	Dav	New York	70	$66,109					
13									

Formula explanation:

=COUNTIFS(State,F2,Orders,G2)

- The criteria_range1 argument references the range B2:B12 for which the range name **State** has been used.

- The criteria1 argument is cell **F2**, which has the State we want to use as our criteria. Using a cell reference here makes it easier to change the value.

  This argument is a relative cell reference because we want it to change (relatively) as we copy the formula to other cells.

- The criteria_range2 is the range C2:C12, which has the range name **Orders** in the worksheet. We will be using criteria2 to evaluate this range.

- The criteria2 argument is **G2**, which is the expression **>=40**. A cell reference is used for this argument to make it easier to change the criteria.

We enter the formula in cell **H2** and copy it down the column to count the number of people with orders that match the criteria for each state.

COUNTA Function

The COUNTA function counts the number of cells that are not empty in a group of cells or range. The difference between the COUNTA and COUNT is that COUNTA counts all cells containing an entry, including empty text ("") and even error values. COUNT, on the other hand, only counts cells that contain numeric values.

Syntax

=COUNTA(value1, [value2], ...)

Arguments

Argument	Description
value1	Required. The first argument represents the range in which you want to count cells with an entry.
value2, ...	Optional. You can have additional value arguments up to a maximum of 255 arguments in total.

Remarks

- If you want to count only cells that contain numeric values, use the COUNT function.

- Use the COUNTIF function or the COUNTIFS function if you only want to count cells that meet certain criteria.

Example

In the following example, we use the COUNTA function to count cells with entries in our range of cells. The group of cells containing our data, A1:D14, is a named range called *Orders_Range*.

The COUNTA function is demonstrated next to other functions like COUNT and COUNTBLANK to show the difference in the results.

Formula: =COUNTA(Orders_Range)

Result: 37

	Orders_Range		fx	Orders	
	A	B	C	D	E
1	**Orders**				
2		**Customer**	**Order Date**	**Order Total**	
3	**Sector 1**	Bruce Henderson	1/15/2022	$2,635	
4		Louis Anderson	2/2/2022	$7,227	
5		Earl Foster	3/3/2022	$4,426	
6		Sean Hill	4/4/2022	$8,774	
7					
8	**Sector 2**	Benjamin Martinez	4/12/2022	$9,829	
9		Joe Perez	4/15/2022	$2,194	
10		Shawn Johnson	4/17/2022	$2,459	
11		Kenneth Roberts	5/8/2022	$3,920	
12		Cynthia Martin	5/19/2022	$2,566	
13		Susan Mitchell	6/10/2022	$7,034	
14				$51,064	
15					
16	Total # cells	56	=ROWS(Orders_Range)*COLUMNS(Orders_Range)		
17	**Occupied cells**	37	=COUNTA(Orders_Range)		
18	Numeric values	21	=COUNT(Orders_Range)		
19	Blank cells	19	=COUNTBLANK(Orders_Range)		
20					

COUNTBLANK Function

The COUNTBLANK function counts the number of empty cells in a range.

Syntax

=COUNTBLANK(range)

Argument	Description
range	Required. The first argument represents the range in which you want to count the blank cells.

Cells with formulas that return an empty string ("") are also counted. Cells with 0 (zero) are not counted.

Example

In the following example, we use the COUNTBLANK function to count the blank cells in the range A1:D14 named *Orders_Range*.

Formula: =COUNTBLANK(Orders_Range)

Result: 19

	A	B	C	D	E
1	Orders				
2		Customer	Order Date	Order Total	
3	Sector 1	Bruce Henderson	1/15/2022	$2,635	
4		Louis Anderson	2/2/2022	$7,227	
5		Earl Foster	3/3/2022	$4,426	
6		Sean Hill	4/4/2022	$8,774	
7					
8	Sector 2	Benjamin Martinez	4/12/2022	$9,829	
9		Joe Perez	4/15/2022	$2,194	
10		Shawn Johnson	4/17/2022	$2,459	
11		Kenneth Roberts	5/8/2022	$3,920	
12		Cynthia Martin	5/19/2022	$2,566	
13		Susan Mitchell	6/10/2022	$7,034	
14				$51,064	
15					
16	Total # cells	56	=ROWS(Orders_Range)*COLUMNS(Orders_Range)		
17	Occupied cells	37	=COUNTA(Orders_Range)		
18	Numeric values	21	=COUNT(Orders_Range)		
19	Blank cells	19	=COUNTBLANK(Orders_Range)		
20					

Calculating Averages and Extreme Values

The functions in this section enable you to create formulas that return the average, median, and extreme values like maximum and minimum values. You can also use corresponding advanced functions to create formulas that evaluate only a subset of values based on the criteria you provide.

AVERAGE Function

The AVERAGE function is one of the widely used aggregate functions in Excel. It returns the average of the arguments. The average is the arithmetic mean of a series of numbers and is calculated by adding up the numbers and then dividing by the count of those numbers.

Syntax

=AVERAGE(number1, [number2], ...)

Arguments

Argument	Description
number1	Required. The first cell reference, range, or number for which you want to calculate an average.
number2, ...	Optional. Additional cell references, ranges, or numbers for which you want to calculate an average up to a maximum of 255.

Remarks

- Arguments can include numbers, named ranges, or cell references containing numbers.

- If any of the cells referenced in the arguments contain an error value, AVERAGE returns an error.

- Text, logical values, and empty cells are ignored, but cells with the value zero (0) are included.

- Use the AVERAGEA function to include logical values and text representations of numbers as part of the calculation.

- Use AVERAGEIF and AVERAGEIFS to calculate the average of a subset of values that meet a set of criteria.

Example

In the example below, we use the AVERAGE function to calculate the average of the scores in C2:C16.

Formula

=AVERAGE(C2:C16)

	F2		⌄	⋮	✕	✓	*fx*	=AVERAGE(C2:C16)	

	A	B	C	D	E	F
1	**Student**	**Subject**	**Score**		**Average score**	
2	Bruce	Math	75		All subjects	64.7
3	Louis	Chemistry	61			
4	Earl	Biology	67			
5	Sean	English	74			
6	Benjamin	Math	86			
7	Joe	Chemistry	58			
8	Shawn	Biology	74			
9	Kenneth	English	70			
10	Cynthia	Math	55			
11	Susan	Chemistry	49			
12	John	Math	76			
13	Bruce	English	60			
14	Louis	Biology	68			
15	Earl	Chemistry	47			
16	Kenneth	Math	50			
17						

AVERAGEIF Function

The AVERAGEIF function is a combination of a statistical function and a logical function. AVERAGEIF returns the average (or arithmetic mean) of all the cells in a range that meet a specified condition.

Syntax

=AVERAGEIF(range, criteria, [average_range])

Arguments

Argument	Description
range	Required. A reference to one or more cells to average. This argument can include numbers, cell references, or named ranges.
criteria	Required. An expression that determines which cells are included in the average.
average_range	Optional. The actual set of cells to average, if not the cells in the *range* argument. If this argument is omitted, *range* is used.

Remarks

- AVERAGEIF will return the error #DIV/0! if no cells in *range* meet the criteria.

- AVERAGEIF will return the error #DIV/0! if *range* is a blank or text string.

- If a cell in *criteria* is empty, it is treated as zero (0).

- Cells in the range argument that contain logical values like TRUE or FALSE are ignored.

- You can use wildcard characters like the question mark (?) and asterisk (*) in your criteria to find matches that are similar but not the same. A question mark matches any single character, while an asterisk matches a sequence of characters. To find a character like a question mark or asterisk, type a tilde sign (~) in front of the character.

- *Average_range* does not necessarily need to be the same number of rows and columns as *range*. The average is performed by using the top-left cell in average_range plus cells that match the same number of rows and columns in the range argument. See examples in the table below:

range	average_range	Cells evaluated and averaged
A1:A10	B1:B10	B1:B10
A1:A10	B1:B5	B1:B10
A1:B5	C1:C3	C1:D5

Example

In the following example, we use the AVERAGEIF function to calculate the average test scores for students per subject. We want to group the data by **Subject** (for example, Biology, Chemistry, Math, etc.) and average each group by **Score**.

The range used to filter the averaged data is B2:B16, and the range that averaged is C2:C16. The formula uses range names for the referenced ranges to make them absolute references.

F2			fx	=AVERAGEIF(Subjects,E2,Scores)		
	A	B	C	D	E	F	G

	A	B	C	D	E	F	G
1	Student	Subject	Score		Subject	Average	Formula text
2	Bruce	Math	75		Math	68.4	=AVERAGEIF(Subjects,E2,Scores)
3	Louis	Chemistry	61		Chemistry	53.8	=AVERAGEIF(Subjects,E3,Scores)
4	Earl	Biology	67		English	68.0	=AVERAGEIF(Subjects,E4,Scores)
5	Sean	English	74		Biology	69.7	=AVERAGEIF(Subjects,E5,Scores)
6	Benjamin	Math	86				
7	Joe	Chemistry	58				
8	Shawn	Biology	74				
9	Kenneth	English	70				
10	Cynthia	Math	55				
11	Susan	Chemistry	49				
12	John	Math	76		*Subjects = B2:B16*		
13	Bruce	English	60		*Scores = C2:C16*		
14	Louis	Biology	68				
15	Earl	Chemistry	47				
16	Kenneth	Math	50				
17							

Formula explanation:

=AVERAGEIF(Subjects,E2,Scores)

Subjects = B2:B16
Scores = C2:C16

- The range argument references cells B2:B16 (named Subjects), which is used to filter the values to be averaged.

- The criteria argument is **E2**, which is a reference to our criteria. Using a cell reference makes it easier to change the criteria on the worksheet. This argument is a relative reference because we want the criteria to change (relatively) as we copy the formula to other cells.

- The average_range argument references cells C2:C16 (named Scores), which is the range we want to average based on the criteria.

We enter the formula in cell F2 to return the average for Math, then copy the formula to cells F3:F5 to display the average for the other subjects.

AVERAGEIFS Function

The AVERAGEIFS function returns the average (arithmetic mean) of all cells that meet a set of criteria. This function allows you to specify several criteria pairs to select the data to be included in the average. An IFS function enables you to create several range/criteria pairs to select the data that meet the criteria.

The function identifies items that meet the criteria in one column and averages corresponding items in another. You can have up to a maximum of 127 range/criteria pairs, as you can only have 255 arguments in an Excel function.

Syntax

=AVERAGEIFS(average_range, criteria_range1, criteria1, [criteria_range2, criteria2], ...)

Arguments

Argument	Description
average_range	Required. The range of cells for which you want the average calculated.
criteria_range1	Required. The range to evaluate using criteria1.
criteria1	Required. The criteria used to evaluate criteria1_range to select matching data. For example, criteria can be entered as 40, ">40", C6, "bolts", or "125".
Criteria_range2, criteria2, …	Optional. You can have additional range/criteria pairs, up to 127 total pairs.

Example

This example shows a list of orders from different sales reps for several states. We want to find the average sales per state for entries with 10 or more orders (>=10).

We can use the following formula to achieve the result:

=AVERAGEIFS(Sales,States,F2,Orders,G2)

Sales = D2:D12
States = B2:B12
Orders = C2:C12

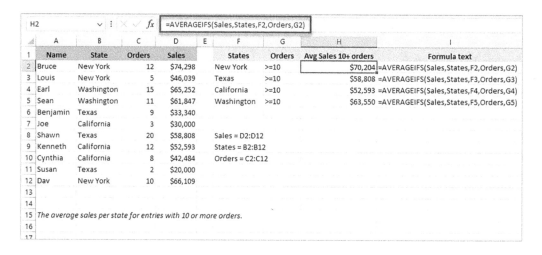

H2			f_x	=AVERAGEIFS(Sales,States,F2,Orders,G2)				
	A	B	C	D	E	F	G	H	I
1	Name	State	Orders	Sales		States	Orders	Avg Sales 10+ orders	Formula text
2	Bruce	New York	12	$74,298		New York	>=10	$70,204	=AVERAGEIFS(Sales,States,F2,Orders,G2)
3	Louis	New York	5	$46,039		Texas	>=10	$58,808	=AVERAGEIFS(Sales,States,F3,Orders,G3)
4	Earl	Washington	15	$65,252		California	>=10	$52,593	=AVERAGEIFS(Sales,States,F4,Orders,G4)
5	Sean	Washington	11	$61,847		Washington	>=10	$63,550	=AVERAGEIFS(Sales,States,F5,Orders,G5)
6	Benjamin	Texas	9	$33,340					
7	Joe	California	3	$30,000					
8	Shawn	Texas	20	$58,808		Sales = D2:D12			
9	Kenneth	California	12	$52,593		States = B2:B12			
10	Cynthia	California	8	$42,484		Orders = C2:C12			
11	Susan	Texas	2	$20,000					
12	Dav	New York	10	$66,109					
13									
14									
15	The average sales per state for entries with 10 or more orders.								
16									
17									

Formula explanation:

=AVERAGEIFS(Sales,States,F2,Orders,G2)

- The average_range argument references D2:D12 (named Sales), the range for which we calculate the average.

- The criteria_range1 is B2:B12 for which a range name States has been used.

- The criteria1 argument is F2, a cell reference to the value used as the criteria. A cell reference makes it easier to change the criteria on the worksheet.

    This argument is a relative reference as we want it to change as we copy the formula to other cells.

- The criteria_range2 argument is C2:C12 (named Orders) has been used.

- The criteria2 argument is cell G2, which references our criteria (>=10). This argument is a matching pair for criteria_range2. A cell reference has been used to make it easier to change the criteria if needed.

The first criteria_range/criteria pair filters the data by State, and the second criteria_range/criteria pair filters the data by Orders. The formula then returns the average of the filtered data.

The formula is entered in cell H2 and copied to H3:H5 to calculate the average for the other states.

MAX, MIN, and MEDIAN Functions

The MAX, MIN, and MEDIAN functions are some of the most commonly used functions in Excel and are very similar in their arguments and usage. In a set of values, MAX returns the largest number, MIN returns the smallest number, and MEDIAN returns the number in the middle. We can cover these functions simultaneously as they're similar in arguments.

Syntax

=MAX(number1, [number2], ...)

=MIN(number1, [number2], ...)

=MEDIAN(number1, [number2], ...)

Arguments – similar for all three functions

Argument	Description
Number1	Required. A number, range, array, or cell reference that contains numbers.
number2, ...	Optional. You can have additional numbers, cell references, or ranges up to a maximum of 255 arguments that you want to evaluate.

Remarks

- MEDIAN calculates the average of the two middle numbers if there is an even number of values.

- The functions will return 0 (zero) if the arguments contain no numbers.

- Excel uses only the numbers in a reference or array argument. Logical values, text values, and empty cells in the reference or array are ignored.

- The functions will return an error if arguments contain error values or text that cannot be translated into numbers.

- Text representations of numbers and logical values that you directly type into the arguments list are counted.

- Use the MAXA and MINA functions if you want to include logical values and text representations of numbers as part of the result for MAX and MIN. You can search for the MAXA or MINA with the **Insert Function** command on Excel's Formulas tab.

Example

The example below shows the maximum, minimum, and median values for the **Sales** column (D2:D12).

The following formulas return the desired results:

- MAX(D2:D12)

- MIN(D2:D12)

- MEDIAN(D2:D12)

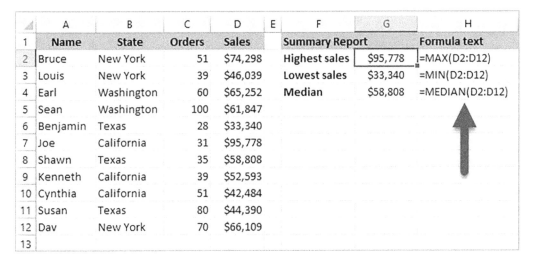

	A	B	C	D	E	F	G	H
1	Name	State	Orders	Sales		Summary Report		Formula text
2	Bruce	New York	51	$74,298		Highest sales	$95,778	=MAX(D2:D12)
3	Louis	New York	39	$46,039		Lowest sales	$33,340	=MIN(D2:D12)
4	Earl	Washington	60	$65,252		Median	$58,808	=MEDIAN(D2:D12)
5	Sean	Washington	100	$61,847				
6	Benjamin	Texas	28	$33,340				
7	Joe	California	31	$95,778				
8	Shawn	Texas	35	$58,808				
9	Kenneth	California	39	$52,593				
10	Cynthia	California	51	$42,484				
11	Susan	Texas	80	$44,390				
12	Dav	New York	70	$66,109				
13								

To add more cell references or ranges to the arguments, separate them with a comma. For example, MAX(C1:C5, G1:G5).

MAXIFS and MINIFS Functions

The MAXIFS and MINIFS functions are an extension of the MAX and MIN functions to include a conditional component in their functionality. MAXIFS returns the maximum value of all cells that meet the specified criteria. MINIFS returns the minimum value of all cells that meet the specified criteria. You can specify more than one set of criteria to determine which data is selected to be part of the evaluation.

An IFS function enables you to create several range/criteria pairs to narrow down the data to only those that meet the criteria. The functions identify items that meet the criteria in one column and calculate corresponding items in another.

You can have up to a maximum of 127 range/criteria pairs, as you can only have 255 arguments in an Excel function.

Syntax

=MAXIFS(max_range, criteria_range1, criteria1, [criteria_range2, criteria2], ...)

=MINIFS(min_range, criteria_range1, criteria1, [criteria_range2, criteria2], ...)

Arguments – similar for both functions

Argument	Description
max_range (MAX function) min_range(MIN function)	Required. The actual range of cells for which we want the maximum or minimum value determined.
criteria_range1	Required. The range evaluated using criteria1.
criteria1	Required. The criteria used to determine which cells in criteria_range1 will be part of the calculation. This argument can be a number, expression, or text. For example, criteria can be entered as 40, ">40", C6, "bolts", or "125".
criteria_range2, criteria2, ...	Optional. You can have additional range/criteria pairs, up to 127 total pairs.

Remarks

- The max_range (or min_range) and criteria_range arguments must have the same number of rows and columns. Otherwise, these functions return the #VALUE! error.

- The range we use to filter the data does not necessarily have to be the same range from which we want to generate the max or min value.

Example

In this example, we want to produce reports that show the minimum and maximums sales per state. However, we only want to evaluate entries with 10 or more orders (>=10). So, we have different criteria that we want to use to determine the data to be evaluated.

Formulas

The following formulas return the desired results.

Maximum:
=MAXIFS(Sales,States,F3,Orders,G3)

Minimum:
=MINIFS(Sales,States,F10,Orders,G10)

	A	B	C	D	E	F	G	H	I
1	Name	State	Orders	Sales		Max Sales			
2	Bruce	New York	12	$74,298		States	Orders	Max Sales	Formula Text
3	Louis	New York	5	$46,039		New York	>=10	$74,298	=MAXIFS(Sales,States,F3,Orders,G3)
4	Earl	Washington	15	$65,252		Texas	>=10	$58,808	=MAXIFS(Sales,States,F4,Orders,G4)
5	Sean	Washington	11	$61,847		California	>=10	$52,593	=MAXIFS(Sales,States,F5,Orders,G5)
6	Benjamin	Texas	10	$33,340		Washington	>=10	$65,252	=MAXIFS(Sales,States,F6,Orders,G6)
7	Joe	California	3	$30,000					
8	Shawn	Texas	20	$58,808		Min Sales			
9	Kenneth	California	12	$52,593		States	Orders	Min sales	Formula Text
10	Cynthia	California	8	$42,484		New York	>=10	$66,109	=MINIFS(Sales,States,F10,Orders,G10)
11	Susan	Texas	2	$20,000		Texas	>=10	$33,340	=MINIFS(Sales,States,F11,Orders,G11)
12	Dav	New York	10	$66,109		California	>=10	$52,593	=MINIFS(Sales,States,F12,Orders,G12)
13						Washington	>=10	$61,847	=MINIFS(Sales,States,F13,Orders,G13)
14									

Formula explanation

Both functions use identical cell references and criteria arguments. So, they can be described together.

=MAXIFS(Sales,States,F3,Orders,G3)

=MINIFS(Sales,States,F10,Orders,G10)

- The first argument references D2:D12, which has the range name **Sales**. We want to evaluate this range for the maximum and minimum values.

- The criteria_range1 argument is referencing B2:B12 (named **States**). This argument makes up the first range/criteria pair we're using to filter the data to be evaluated.

- The criteria1 argument is **F2**, a cell reference to the criteria - **New York**. Using a cell reference makes it easier to change the criteria.

- The criteria_range2 argument is C2:C12 (named **Orders**). Criteria_range2 is part of the second range/criteria pair.

- The criteria2 argument is cell **G2** which holds the criteria for the number of orders, ">=10". Criteria2 is part of the second range/criteria pair used to filter the data to be evaluated. A cell reference has been used to make it easier to change the criteria.

To display the results, we enter the MAXIFS formula in cell H3 and copy it to the other cells for which we want to display maximum sales. For the minimum values, the MINIFS formula is entered in cell H10 and copied to the other cells displaying the minimum sales.

Chapter 6

Date and Time Functions

This chapter covers functions that enable you to:

- Return the day, month, or year from a given date.

- Add or subtract days, months, and years from dates.

- Combine different values into a single date.

- Return the number of days, months, or years between two dates.

- Convert date values entered as text into recognized Excel dates, for example, in the case of imported data.

- Return the number of whole working days between two dates.

- Return the current date or the date and time.

- Return the decimal number for a given time.

The date and time functions can be found in Excel by clicking the Date & Time command on the Formulas tab on the Ribbon. The dropdown menu lists all the date and time functions in Excel.

Excel stores dates and times as serial numbers internally, for example, 45280.83583. The numbers to the left of the decimal point represent the date, and the numbers to the right of the decimal point represent the time. Excel calculates dates and times using serial numbers like this. Any entry formatted as a date/time in Excel is automatically converted internally into a serial number. For example, by default, 1/1/1900 is serial number 1, and 1/1/2023 is serial number 44927 because 1/1/2023 is 44927 days after 1/1/1900.

Date Formats

Before delving into the date functions, we need to look at date formats in Excel and how to set cells to different date formats. The default date and time formats used by Excel will be the ones you have set in your regional settings in Windows (or macOS for Macs).

The short date format used in Europe is Day/Month/Year (i.e., dd/mm/yy), while in the United States, the short date format is Month/Day/Year (i.e., m/dd/yy).

You can change how dates are displayed in your Excel worksheet regardless of your regional date settings in Windows or macOS.

To change the date format in Excel, do the following:

1. Select the cell(s) for which you want to change the date format.

2. Right-click and select **Format Cells** on the shortcut menu.

3. Under **Category**, select **Date**.

4. Under **Locale (location)**, select the region. For example, English (United States).

5. Under **Type**, select the date format you want.

6. To select a different time format, select **Time** under Category and follow the same steps above to choose a time format.

7. Click OK.

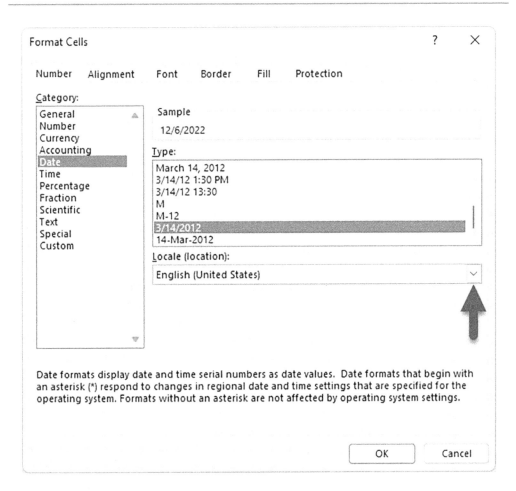

For the examples in this chapter, we will use the United States short date convention **m/d/yyyy**. If you're in a region using the dd/mm/yyyy convention, simply swap the month and day of the dates used in the examples.

Add Days, Months, and Years to a Date

This section covers functions that enable you to add and subtract dates. You can combine date functions to create formulas that add or subtract dates, including days, months, and years.

DAY, MONTH, and YEAR Functions

The DAY, MONTH, and YEAR functions are very similar and are often used together, so this section covers them simultaneously. They all take a single argument, a serial number representing a date.

DAY returns the day (an integer between 1 to 31) corresponding to a date entered as its argument.

MONTH returns the month (an integer between 1 to 12, representing January to December) corresponding to a date entered as its argument.

YEAR returns the year (as an integer in the range 1900-9999) corresponding to a date entered as its argument.

Syntax

=DAY(serial_number)

=MONTH(serial_number)

=YEAR(serial_number)

Argument	Description
Serial_number	Required. All three functions have the same kind of argument. This argument must be a recognized date. It is the date for the day, month, or year you want to return.
	You can use the DATE function in this argument to ensure a proper date is entered, for example, DATE(2019,4,28). Problems may occur if dates are entered as text.

Remarks

The values returned by the YEAR, MONTH, and DAY functions are always Gregorian values regardless of the date format of the argument. For example, if the entered date is Hijri (Islamic Calendar), the values returned by DAY, MONTH, and YEAR will be the equivalent in the Gregorian calendar.

Example 1

In the example below, we use the DAY, MONTH, and YEAR functions to extract the day, month, and year from a given date in cell A1.

Formulas:
    =DAY(A1)
    =MONTH(A1)
    =YEAR(A1)

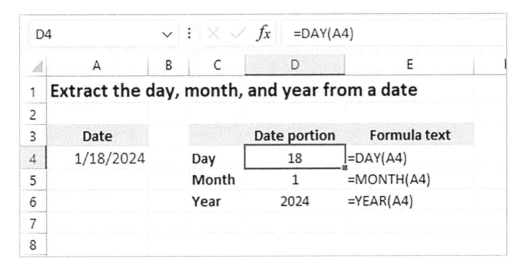

> **Note** In the next section, see examples of how to add or subtract days, months, or years from a date by combining DAY, MONTH, and YEAR with the DATE function.

DATE Function

The DATE function enables you to combine different values into a single date.

Syntax

=DATE (year, month, day)

Arguments

Argument	Description
year	Required. This argument can have one to four digits. Excel uses the date system on your computer to interpret the year argument.
month	Required. The month argument should be a positive or negative integer between 1 to 12, representing January to December. If the month argument is a negative number (*-n*), the function returns a date *n* months from the last month of the previous year. For example, DATE(2019,-4,2) will return the serial number representing August 2, 2018.
day	Required. This argument can be a positive or negative integer from 1 to 31, representing the day of the month.

Remarks

- If the month argument is greater than 12, the function adds that number of months to the last month of the specified year. For example, DATE(2022,14,4) will return the serial number representing February 4, 2023.

- If day is greater than the number of days in the specified month, the function adds that number of days to the first day of the next month of the specified date. For example, DATE(2022,2,30) returns the serial number representing March 2, 2022.

- If day is less than 1, Excel subtracts that number of days from the last day of the previous month. For example, DATE(2022,12,-10) will return the serial number that represents November 20, 2022. Excel subtracted 10 from the 30 days in November, which is the previous month.

- Excel sometimes automatically detects a date entry and formats the cell accordingly. However, if you copied and pasted a date from another source, you may need to manually format the cell to a date to display the date properly.

> **Tip** Always use four digits for the year argument to prevent unwanted results. For example, 04 could mean 1904 or 2004. Using four-digit years prevents any confusion.

Example 1

In this example, we want to combine values from different cells for the month, day, and year into a date value recognized in Excel.

When we use the DATE function to combine values into a single date, we get the following formula:

=DATE(C4,A4,B4)

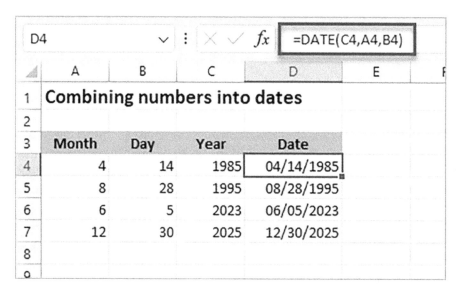

	A	B	C	D
1	Combining numbers into dates			
2				
3	Month	Day	Year	Date
4	4	14	1985	04/14/1985
5	8	28	1995	08/28/1995
6	6	5	2023	06/05/2023
7	12	30	2025	12/30/2025
8				

Example 2

When we combine the DATE function with the DAY, MONTH, and YEAR functions, we can perform the following date calculations:

- Add 5 years to 12/15/2022

- Add 15 months to 12/15/2022

- Add 60 days to 10/15/2022

The image below shows the formulas used to perform these calculations.

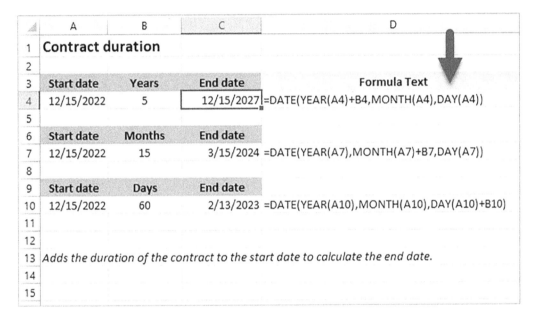

	A	B	C	D
1	Contract duration			
2				
3	Start date	Years	End date	Formula Text
4	12/15/2022	5	12/15/2027	=DATE(YEAR(A4)+B4,MONTH(A4),DAY(A4))
5				
6	Start date	Months	End date	
7	12/15/2022	15	3/15/2024	=DATE(YEAR(A7),MONTH(A7)+B7,DAY(A7))
8				
9	Start date	Days	End date	
10	12/15/2022	60	2/13/2023	=DATE(YEAR(A10),MONTH(A10),DAY(A10)+B10)
11				
12				
13	Adds the duration of the contract to the start date to calculate the end date.			
14				
15				

Formula Explanation

Add 5 years to 12/15/2022

=DATE(YEAR(A4)+B4,MONTH(A4),DAY(A4))

The **year** argument of the DATE function has **YEAR(A4)+B4** (i.e., 2022 + 5, which returns 2027). The other nested functions return the month and day in the **month** and **day** arguments. To subtract years, use the minus sign (−) in place of the plus sign (+) in the formula.

Add 15 Months to 12/15/2022

=DATE(YEAR(A7),MONTH(A7)+B7,DAY(A7))

In this formula, **MONTH(A7)+B7** adds 15 months to the start date. The other nested functions return the year and day, respectively, in the year and day arguments of the DATE function. To subtract months, use the – sign in place of the + sign in the formula.

Add 60 days to 12/15/2022

=DATE(YEAR(A10),MONTH(A10),DAY(A10)+B10)

In this formula, **DAY(A10)+B10** adds 60 days to the start date. The other nested functions return the year and month, respectively, in the year and month arguments of the DATE function. To subtract days, use the – sign in place of the + sign in the formula.

EDATE Function

The EDATE function allows you to add or subtract months from a given date. EDATE is useful for calculating end dates on the same day of the month as the start date.

Syntax

=EDATE(start_date, months)

Arguments

Argument	Description
start_date	Required. This argument should be a date representing the start date. It can be a cell reference or a value. Cell references should have the Date format. Use the DATE function for values directly entered. For example, use DATE(2023,1,25) for January 25, 2023. You may get inconsistent results if dates are entered as text.
months	Required. An integer representing the number of months before or after start_date. A positive value returns a future date, and a negative value returns a date in the past.

Remarks

- If start_date is not a valid date, EDATE will return a #VALUE! error.
- If the months argument is not an integer, it is truncated.

Example

In the following example, we use the EDATE function to calculate the expiry dates for a series of property lease contracts with start dates (A3:A15) and lease lengths in months (B3:B15).

Formula:

=EDATE(A3,B3)

The formula was entered in cell A3 and copied to the other cells in the column with the fill handle.

C3		∨ ⋮ ✕ ✓ 𝑓𝑥	=EDATE(A3,B3)
◢	A	B	C
1	**Property Lease**		
2	**Start Date**	**Length (Months)**	**Expiry Date**
3	1/28/2023	24	1/28/2025
4	4/4/2023	12	4/4/2024
5	4/16/2023	12	4/16/2024
6	5/21/2023	24	5/21/2025
7	5/28/2023	36	5/28/2026
8	10/27/2023	6	4/27/2024
9	11/9/2023	24	11/9/2025
10	12/7/2023	12	12/7/2024
11	12/14/2023	24	12/14/2025
12	2/21/2024	36	2/21/2027
13	5/6/2024	6	11/6/2024
14	7/25/2024	24	7/25/2026
15	11/29/2024	12	11/29/2025
16			
17			

Note that the cells in A3:A15 and C3:C15 were set to the **Date** format so that Excel displays the dates properly.

NOW Function

The NOW function returns the current date and time. It's a straightforward function with no arguments. The function displays the date using the date and time format of your regional settings. Check the **Date Formats** section of this book for how to change the date format of a cell.

You can use the NOW function to display the current date and time in a cell and have it updated every time you open the worksheet. You can also use the NOW function as arguments in other functions to calculate dates based on the current date and time.

Syntax

=NOW()

Remarks

- The results of the NOW function are not continuously updated. It only updates when the worksheet is recalculated, i.e., when new values or formulas are entered or a macro that contains the function is run.

- If the cell containing the NOW function was changed to a General format, it would display the current date as a serial number, for instance, 43454.83583. Numbers to the left of the decimal point represent the date, and numbers to the right represent the time. For example, serial number 0.5 represents the time 12:00 noon.

Example

In the example below, the NOW function is used in different formulas to display date calculations based on the current date and time.

Formulas:
> =NOW()
> =NOW()-10.5
> =NOW()+10
> =NOW()+2.25
> =EDATE(NOW(),3)

	A	B	C
1	Result	Formula text	Description
2	09/07/2022 13:19	=NOW()	Returns the current date and time
3	44811.55532	=NOW()	Returns the current date and time (General Number cell format)
4	08/28/2022 01:19	=NOW()-10.5	Returns the date and time 10 days and 12 hours ago (-10.5 days ago)
5	09/17/2022 13:19	=NOW()+10	Returns the date and time 10 days in the future
6	09/09/2022 19:19	=NOW()+2.25	Returns the date and time 2 days and 6 hours in the future
7	12/07/2022 00:00	=EDATE(NOW(),3)	3 months in the future, time removed
8			

TODAY Function

The TODAY function returns the serial number of the current date. When you use this function, Excel automatically changes the cell's number format to a **Date**, which displays the value as a date instead of a serial number. To see the date value as a serial number, you must change the cell format to **General** or Number.

The TODAY function is useful for displaying the current date on a worksheet. The function is also useful for calculating the difference between dates. For instance, you can calculate the number of years between two dates by combining the TODAY and YEAR functions.

= YEAR(TODAY())-1979

The formula above uses the TODAY function as an argument in the YEAR function to return the current year. The formula then subtracts 1979 from the current year to return the number of years between 1979 and today.

Syntax

=TODAY()

Example

In the example below, the TODAY function is used in different formulas to display the current date and to calculate other dates based on today's date.

Formulas:
    =TODAY()
    =TODAY()+10
    =DAY(TODAY())
    =MONTH(TODAY())
    =YEAR(TODAY())-2000

	A	B	C
1	Result	Formula text	Description
2	9/7/2022	=TODAY()	Returns the current date.
3	9/17/2022	=TODAY()+10	Returns the current date plus 10 days.
4	7	=DAY(TODAY())	Returns the current day of the month (1 - 31).
5	9	=MONTH(TODAY())	Returns the current month of the year (1 - 12).
6	22	= YEAR(TODAY())-2000	TODAY is used in YEAR to calculate the number of years between the current date and the subtracted date.
7			
8			
9			

📝 Note

If the TODAY function does not update when you open the worksheet, you might need to change the settings in Excel that determine when the workbook recalculates.

If your worksheet is not recalculating, you can enable the automatic calculation option in Excel Options:

1. Click **File** > **Options** > **Formulas** to display the Formulas tab of the Excel Options dialog.

2. Under **Calculation options**, select **Automatic** (if it is not already selected).

Calculate the Difference between Two Dates

The functions in this category enable you to create formulas that calculate the difference between two dates. For example, the number of days, months, or years between a start and an end date.

DATEDIF Function

The DATEDIF function calculates the difference between two dates. This function provides one of the easiest ways in Excel to calculate the difference between two dates. It can return the number of days, months, or years between two dates.

DATEDIF is a "hidden" function in Excel because you'll not find it on the list of date functions or when you search for it using the Insert Function dialog box. You must enter it manually any time you want to use it. It is a legacy function from Lotus 1-2-3, but it has been operational on all versions of Excel.

Syntax

=DATEDIF(start_date, end_date, unit)

Arguments

Argument	Description
start_date	Required. This argument represents the start date of the period.
end_date	Required. This argument represents the end date of the period.
unit	Required. This argument represents the unit of measurement you want to return - days, months, or years. It should be entered as a string.
	It can be one of Y, M, D, YM, or YD:
	"Y" = Calculates the number of years in the period.
	"M" = Calculates the number of months in the period.
	"D" = Calculates the number of days in the period.
	"YM" = Calculates the difference between the months in start_date and end_date. The days and years of the dates are ignored.
	"YD"= Calculates the difference between the days of start_date and end_date. The years of the dates are ignored.

Remarks

This function also has an "MD" argument that calculates the number of days while ignoring the month and years. However, Microsoft no longer recommends using the MD argument because, under some conditions, it could return a negative number, which would be an incorrect value.

Example 1

The example below calculates the age from the date of birth of different people.

Formula:

=DATEDIF(A2,TODAY(),"Y")

B2			✓ : ✕ ✓	*fx*	=DATEDIF(A2,TODAY(),"Y")		
	A	B		C	D	E	F
1	**Date of Birth**	**Years**					
2	1/8/1957	65					
3	1/12/1965	57					
4	12/1/1980	41					
5	11/6/1992	29					
6	7/26/2001	21					
7							

The formula combines the DATEDIF function with the TODAY function to get the desired result. The TODAY function returns today's date, so this formula will always use today's date to calculate the age. The "Y" argument returns the difference in years.

Example 2

To calculate the number of months between two dates, we use the "M" argument of the DATEDIF function.

=DATEDIF(A2,B2,"M")

C11		fx	=DATEDIF(A11,B11,"M")	
	A	B	C	D	E
10	**Start Date**	**End Date**	**Months**		
11	12/1/2022	12/1/2023	12		
12	12/1/2022	12/1/2024	24		
13	12/1/2022	6/1/2025	30		
14	12/6/2024	12/1/2027	35		
15	12/6/2023	12/1/2028	59		
16					

DAYS Function

The DAYS function returns the number of days between two dates.

Syntax

=DAYS (end_date, start_date)

Arguments

Argument	Description
end_date	Required. A date that represents the end date of the period.
start_date	Required. A date that represents the start date of the period.

Example

The table below calculates the difference between two dates in several examples.

Formula:

=DAYS(B2, A2)

If you're entering the dates directly into the function, you need to enclose them in quotation marks.

For example:

=DAYS("12/01/2023","12/01/2022") will return 365 days.

NETWORKDAYS Function

The NETWORKDAYS function returns the number of whole working days between two dates. Working days exclude weekends and any dates specified in the holidays argument. You can use NETWORKDAYS to calculate employee pay and other benefits based on the number of days worked in a specific period.

Syntax

=NETWORKDAYS(start_date, end_date, [holidays])

Arguments

Argument	Description
start_date	Required. A date that represents the start date.
end_date	Required. A date that represents the end date.
holidays	Optional. A range, list, or table with one or more dates to be excluded from the working calendar, for example, state holidays, federal holidays, and floating holidays.

Remarks

If you're entering a date directly as an argument, you should use the DATE function to ensure the argument is converted to a date. For example, use DATE(2023,5,23) instead of "May 23, 2023". Problems can occur if dates are entered as text. If you are referencing a date in a cell, ensure the date format is applied to the cell.

Example

The example below uses the NETWORKDAYS function to calculate the workdays between the project start and end dates. The worksheet also has a range named **Holiday_range** used for the holidays argument. Holiday_range contains the holiday dates to exclude from the count of workdays.

Formula:

=NETWORKDAYS(A4,B4,Holidays_range)

| C4 | | | f_x | =NETWORKDAYS(A4,B4,Holidays_range) |

	A	B	C	D
1	**Projects - Workdays**			
2				
3	**Start date**	**End date**	**Workdays**	**Formula text**
4	2/1/2023	2/1/2024	259	=NETWORKDAYS(A4,B4,Holidays_range)
5	4/1/2023	4/1/2024	258	=NETWORKDAYS(A5,B5,Holidays_range)
6	6/1/2023	6/1/2024	259	=NETWORKDAYS(A6,B6,Holidays_range)
7				
8	**Holidays**			
9	1/2/2023			*Holidays_range = A9:A13*
10	7/4/2023			
11	12/25/2023			
12	1/2/2024			
13	7/4/2024			
14				

The answers are displayed under **Workdays** in the table.

Column D displays the formulas in range C4:C6 (Workdays).

> **Tip** If you want to be able to specify weekend days that are different from the default Saturday and Sunday used in the Gregorian calendar, use the NETWORKDAYS.INTL function instead of NETWORKDAYS.

To access the NETWORKDAYS.INTL function, on the Ribbon, click **Formulas > Date & Time > NETWORKDAYS.INTL**.

Convert Values to Date and Time

The functions discussed in this section enable you to create formulas that convert values in other formats to Excel date and time formats. These formulas are useful for combining values from different cells into one date or time value.

DATEVALUE Function

The DATEVALUE function converts a date entered as text to a serial number in Excel that is recognized as a date. The DATEVALUE function is useful when a worksheet contains dates imported from another application, and Excel reads that data as text. In those instances, you must convert the values to recognized dates in Excel to perform date calculations. Once the values have been converted to dates, you can sort, filter, add, or subtract dates.

DATEVALUE returns a serial number internally recognized as a date. To format this number as a date, you must apply a **Date** format to the cell. For example, the formula =DATEVALUE("1/1/2023") returns 44927, its internal serial number. A cell formatted as a date will display the value as 1/1/2023.

Syntax

=DATEVALUE(date_text)

Arguments

Argument	Description
date_text	Required. Text that represents a date in an Excel date format or a cell reference containing text that represents a date in an Excel date format. For example, "1/30/2008" or "30-Jan-2008" are text strings in quotation marks representing dates.

Remarks

- The date_text argument must represent a date between January 1, 1900, and December 31, 9999. DATEVALUE will return an error if the date_text argument falls outside this range.

- If you omit the year part of the date in the date_text argument, the DATEVALUE function will use the current year from your computer's internal clock.

Example

The following example converts several date textual values to serial numbers using the DATEVALUE function.

C2		fx	=DATEVALUE(A2)	
	A	B	C	D
1	Date as Text	General number format	Date format (US)	Formula text
2	22 May 2011	40685	5/22/2011	=DATEVALUE(A2)
3	5 Jul	44747	7/5/2022	=DATEVALUE(A3)
4	01/01/2023	44927	1/1/2023	=DATEVALUE(A4)
5	April 1990	32964	4/1/1990	=DATEVALUE(A5)
6				

Formula Explanation

=DATEVALUE(A2)

- In the image above, the cells in column A have the text format, the cells in column B have the general number format, and the cells in column C have the date format.

- The DATEVALUE function has been used to convert the text values in A2:A5 to date values in B2:B5. The results are displayed as date serial numbers because the cells have the General number format.

- The DATEVALUE function has been used to convert the text values from A2:A5 to date values in C2:C5. However, Excel displays the same results as dates because the **Date** format was applied to the range.

TIME Function

The TIME function returns the decimal number representing a specified time. Excel stores dates and times as serial numbers internally.

Example: 43454.83583

The numbers to the left of the decimal point represent the date, and the numbers to the right of the decimal point represent the time. The TIME function will return a decimal number ranging from 0 to 0.99988426, representing the times from 0:00:00 (12:00:00 AM) to 23:59:59 (11:59:59 PM). If a cell had the General format before the function was entered, Excel formats the result as a date to properly display the time instead of a decimal number.

Syntax

TIME(hour, minute, second)

Arguments

Arguments	Descriptions
Hour	Required. This argument can be a number from 0 (zero) to 32767, representing the hour. Any value larger than 23 will be divided by 24, and the remainder will be treated as the hour value. For example, TIME(29,0,0) = TIME(5,0,0) = .20833 or 5:00 AM.
Minute	Required. This argument can be a number from 0 to 32767, representing the minute. Any value larger than 59 will be divided by 60 and converted to hours and minutes. For example, TIME(0,810,0) = TIME(13,30,0) = .5625 or 1:30 PM.
Second	Required. This argument can be a number from 0 to 32767, representing the second. Any value larger than 59 will be divided by 60 and converted to hours, minutes, and seconds. For example, TIME(0,0,2120) = TIME(0,35,22) = .02456 or 0:35:22 AM

Example

In this example, the range B3:C4 has values for Hour, Minute, and Second that we want to use for our calculation. E3:E4 and F3:F4 show the results of using the TIME function to combine the values into a single date value.

Formulas:

=TIME(A3,B3,C3)

=TIME(A4,B4,C4)

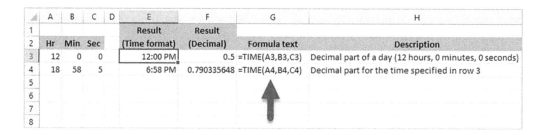

Column E shows the results as times because Excel automatically applies the **Time** format to a cell as it knows the TIME function returns a time.

Column F shows the results as decimal values because the cell Number format was set to General.

Chapter 7

Text Functions

This chapter covers functions that enable you to:

- Find one text string within another one.

- Extract a portion of text from the right, middle, or left of another string.

- Extract a portion of a string based on a character or space within the string.

- Combine values from multiple ranges or strings into one string.

- Trim text by removing all extra spaces except single spaces between words.

- Convert text to uppercase, lowercase, or proper case.

The text functions in Excel can be found by going to **Formulas > Function Library > Text** on the Ribbon. The drop-down menu lists all the text functions in Excel. Text functions are useful for manipulating and rearranging text values.

For example, when you import data into Excel from other applications, you may encounter irregular text spacing or data with the wrong case. You may want to remove extra spaces from the data or change the case to uppercase or lowercase.

> **-Tip**
> The **Flash Fill** command on the Home tab enables you to automatically perform many text manipulation tasks for which you previously needed functions. To learn more about Flash Fill, see my Excel 2022 Basics book.

Find and Extract Substrings

The functions in this category enable you to create formulas that can extract a substring from the left, right, or middle of a string. Support functions like FIND, TRIM, and LEN are often combined with other text functions to manipulate text. Recently introduced text functions allow you to perform tasks for which you previously needed to combine several functions.

TEXTBEFORE Function

The TEXTBEFORE function returns text that occurs before a given delimiter or string. If multiple instances of a delimiter exist in the text, you can specify which instance to use for the text portion extraction. TEXTBEFORE offers the same functionality (and more) to handle tasks previously needing a combination of the LEFT and FIND functions.

> **Note** This function is currently only available in Excel for Microsoft 365.

Syntax

=TEXTBEFORE(text,delimiter,[instance_num],   [match_mode],   [match_end], [if_not_found])

Arguments

Argument	Description
text	Required. A value or cell reference representing the text from which you want to extract a substring.
delimiter	Required. The character or text marking the point you want to extract text before.
instance_num	Optional. The instance of the delimiter marking the end point from which you want to extract the text. Use when *text* has more than one instance of *delimiter*, and you want an instance other than the first. The first delimiter instance is 1 (default), the second is 2, and so on. A negative number starts the search from the end.
match_mode	Optional. Determines if the delimiter match is case-sensitive. 0 = case-sensitive; 1= case-insensitive. The default is case-sensitive if omitted.
match_end	Optional. You can enable this option to treat the end of the text as the delimiter for instances where the delimiter is not found. 0 = disabled; 1 = Enabled The default is disabled if omitted.
if_not_found	Optional. Specifies the value to return if no match is found. If this argument is omitted and no match is found, the default returned is #N/A.

Remarks

- TEXTBEFORE returns a #VALUE! error if instance_num is 0 or greater than the length of text.

- TEXTBEFORE returns a #N/A error if the specified delimiter is not in text.

- TEXTBEFORE returns a #N/A error if the value entered for the instance_num argument exceeds the number of occurrences of delimiter in text.

Examples

The examples in the image below use TEXTBEFORE (in column B) to extract part of the string in column A. The formulas are shown in column C.

	B2		✓ ⋮ ✕ ✓	fx =TEXTBEFORE(A2," ")	

⊿	A	B	C	D
1	**Text**	**Extracted text**	**Formula text**	**Description**
2	Linda Mitchell	Linda	=TEXTBEFORE(A2," ")	Finds space as delimiter
3	Christina Taylor, Analyst	Christina Taylor	=TEXTBEFORE(A3,",")	Finds comma as delimiter
4	Sanchez, Shawn, Manager	Sanchez, Shawn	=TEXTBEFORE(A4,",",2)	Find 2nd comma as delimiter
5	Andrew Steven James	Andrew Steven	=TEXTBEFORE(A5," ",2)	Finds 2nd space as delimiter
6	NWTCFV-91	NWTCFV	=TEXTBEFORE(A6,"-")	Finds dash as delimiter
7	Connecticut - CT	Connecticut	=TEXTBEFORE(A7," - ")	Finds dash and space
8	GTECH-365-4001	GTECH-365	=TEXTBEFORE(A8,"-",2)	Finds 2nd instance of dash
9	GTECH-365-4002-402	GTECH-365-4002	=TEXTBEFORE(A9,"-",-1)	Starts search from the end
10	15 x 45 x 30	15 x 45	=TEXTBEFORE(A10," x ",2)	Finds 2nd instance of x
11				
12				
13				

Formula explanations

=TEXTBEFORE(A2," ")

This formula has A2 as the text from which to extract a substring. The delimiter is a space specified by the double quotes.

=TEXTBEFORE(A3,",")

The delimiter here is a comma.

=TEXTBEFORE(A4,",",2)

The text is in A4, and the delimiter is a comma. The instance_num is 2, which matches the second instance of a comma.

=TEXTBEFORE(A7," - ")

The delimiter is a hyphen with a space on both sides.

=TEXTBEFORE(A8,"-",2)

The delimiter here is a hyphen, and we want to extract all text before the second instance of a hyphen.

=TEXTBEFORE(A9,"-",-1)

The delimiter here is a hyphen. The instance_num is -1, which searches for the first hyphen starting from the end of the text. The formula then returns all text before the hyphen.

=TEXTBEFORE(A10," x ",2)

The delimiter here is a lowercase x bordered by two spaces. The instance_num is 2, which means the formula finds the second instance of x and returns all text before it.

TEXTAFTER Function

The TEXTAFTER function returns text that occurs after a specified delimiter or substring. If multiple instances of a delimiter exist in the text, you can specify which instance to use for the text extraction. You can use TEXTAFTER in instances where you would have previously needed to combine the RIGHT, FIND, and LEN functions to achieve the same result.

> **Note** This function is currently only available in Excel for Microsoft 365.

Syntax

=TEXTAFTER(text,delimiter,[instance_num], [match_mode], [match_end], [if_not_found])

Arguments

Argument	Description
text	Required. A value or cell reference representing the text from which you want to extract a substring.
delimiter	Required. This argument is a character or text marking the point after which you want to extract text.
instance_num	Optional. The instance of the delimiter marking the point after which you want to extract the text. Use when *text* has more than one instance of *delimiter*, and you want an instance other than the first. The first delimiter instance is 1 (default), the second is 2, and so on. A negative number starts the search from the end of the list.
match_mode	Optional. Determines if the delimiter match is case-sensitive. 0 = case-sensitive; 1= case-insensitive.

	The default is case-sensitive if omitted.
match_end	Optional. Treats the end of the text as the delimiter, for example, where the delimiter is not found.
	0 = disabled; 1 = Enabled.
if_not_found	Optional. Specifies the value to return if no match is found. If this argument is omitted and no match is found, the default returned is #N/A.

Remarks

- TEXTAFTER returns a #VALUE! error if instance_num is 0 or greater than the length of *text*.

- TEXTAFTER returns a #N/A error if the specified delimiter is not in *text*.

- TEXTAFTER will return a #N/A error if instance_num is greater than the number of instances of delimiter in *text*.

Examples

The examples in the image below use TEXTAFTER (in column B) to extract part of the string in column A. The formulas are displayed in column C.

	A	B	C	D
1	**Text**	**Extracted**	**Formula text**	**Description**
2	Linda Mitchell	Mitchell	=TEXTAFTER(A2," ")	Finds space as delimiter
3	Sanchez, Shawn	Shawn	=TEXTAFTER(A3,", ")	Find comma and space as delimiter
4	Delaware - DE	DE	=TEXTAFTER(A4," - ")	Finds dash and space
5	NWTCFV-91	91	=TEXTAFTER(A5,"-")	Finds dash as delimiter
6	GTX-365-PH	PH	=TEXTAFTER(A6,"-",2)	Finds 2nd instance of dash
7	15 ft x 10 ft	10 ft	=TEXTAFTER(A7," x ")	Finds x as delimiter
8	Andrew Steven James	Steven	=TEXTBEFORE(TEXTAFTER(A8," ")," ")	Returns text from the middle of the string
9	Minnesota (MN)	MN	=TEXTBEFORE(TEXTAFTER(A9,"("),")")	Returns the abbreviation without the brackets
10	Cora Fabric Chair	Chair	=TEXTAFTER(A10," ",-1)	Returns the first item from the right of the string
11	Habitat Oken Console Table	Table	=TEXTAFTER(A11," ",-1)	Returns the first item from the right of the string
12	Windsor 2 Seater Cuddle Chair	Chair	=TEXTAFTER(A12," ",-1)	Returns the first item from the right of the string
13	Fabric Chair in a Box	Box	=TEXTAFTER(A13," ",-1)	Returns the first item from the right of the string
14				
15				
16				

Formula explanations

=TEXTAFTER(A2," ")

In this formula, A2 is the cell reference to the text from which to extract a substring after the delimiter. The delimiter argument is a space character denoted by a space in quotes.

=TEXTAFTER(A3,", ")

A3 is the cell reference to the text from which to extract a substring after the delimiter. The delimiter argument is a comma and a space character.

=TEXTAFTER(A4," - ")

The delimiter here is a hyphen with a space on each side.

=TEXTAFTER(A5,"-")

The delimiter argument here is a hyphen with no spaces.

=TEXTAFTER(A6,"-",2)

The delimiter argument here is a hyphen. The instance_num is 2, which finds the second instance of a hyphen and returns all text after.

=TEXTAFTER(A7," x ")

The delimiter argument here is a lowercase x with a space character on each side.

=TEXTBEFORE(TEXTAFTER(A8," ")," ")

A8 = Andrew Steven James
Result = Steven

This formula combines TEXTBEFORE and TEXTAFTER to extract the middle name from a full name in cell A8. TEXTAFTER first selects the text after the first space, which is **Steven James**. TEXTBEFORE selects the name before the space in the returned result, **Steven**. This formula provides an easier solution than using the MID and FIND functions to achieve the same result.

=TEXTBEFORE(TEXTAFTER(A9,"("),")")

A9 = Minnesota (MN)
Result = MN

This formula combines TEXTBEFORE and TEXTAFTER to extract the abbreviation from the value in cell A9. TEXTAFTER first returns the text after the opening bracket **MN)**. TEXTBEFORE then returns the characters before the closing bracket, which is **MN**.

=TEXTAFTER(A10," ",-1)

The delimiter argument in the above formula is a space. The instance_num is -1, which tells Excel to find the last space in the text string and return the text after it.

TRIM Function

The TRIM function removes all spaces from a text string causing irregular spacing except for single spaces between words. The TRIM function is useful when you've imported data into Excel from another application, and the text has irregular spacing.

> **Note** The TRIM function does not remove the non-breaking space commonly used in HTML code or web pages - ** **. To remove this type of space, you need to use the Find and Replace function in an HTML editor.

Syntax

=TRIM(text)

Argument	Description
Text	Required. The text you want to trim. This argument can be a text string value or cell reference.

Example

In the following example, we use the TRIM function to remove all extra spaces from the text values in column A.

B2			f_x	=TRIM(A2)

◢	A	B
1	**Category**	**Trimmed**
2	Jams, Preserves	Jams, Preserves
3	Dried Fruit & Nuts	Dried Fruit & Nuts
4	Dried Fruit & Nuts	Dried Fruit & Nuts
5	Canned Fruit & Vegetables	Canned Fruit & Vegetables
6	Baked Goods & Mixes	Baked Goods & Mixes
7	Jams, Preserves	Jams, Preserves
8	Baked Goods & Mixes	Baked Goods & Mixes
9		
10		
11		

LEN Function

The LEN function returns the number of characters in a text string. The LEN function is useful when combined with other Excel functions like RIGHT, LEFT, and MID, where you can use LEN as an argument to return the length of the string from which you want to extract a portion.

Syntax

=LEN(text)

Argument	Description
Text	Required. A text string or a cell reference containing the text for which you want to find the length. Spaces are counted as characters.

Example

In the following example, we use the LEN function to count the number of characters in an item code. The example also demonstrates how the LEN function can be combined with the MID function to return part of a string.

	A	B	C	D
1	Text	Result	Formula text	Description
2	NWTCFV-88	9	=LEN(A2)	Length of item code
3	NWTCFV-90	90	=MID(A3,8,LEN(A3)-7)	MID (used with LEN) extracts only the numbers in the item code
4	NWTCFV-91	NWTCFV	=MID(A4,1,LEN(A4)-3)	MID (used with LEN) extracts only the letters in the item code
5				
6				
7				

FIND Function

The FIND function is used to locate the starting position of one text string within another. It returns the position of the first character of the text you're searching for within the second text. The search is case-sensitive.

Syntax

=FIND(find_text, within_text, [start_num])

Arguments

Argument	Description
find_text	Required. The text you want to find.
within_text	Required. The text string in which you want to find text.
start_num	Optional. Specifies the point from which you want to start the search in within_text. The first character in within_text is 1; the second is 2, etc.
	If you omit this argument, it will start from the first character in within_text.

Example 1

This example uses the FIND function to return the position of different characters in the string "United States." As shown in the results below, the FIND function is case-sensitive.

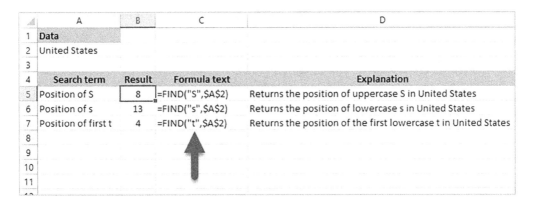

Example 2

The FIND function is most useful when used as an argument in another function. In the following example, we combine FIND with RIGHT, LEFT, and LEN to perform different string extractions. The formulas use FIND to identify the divider's position, then LEFT/RIGHT extracts the portion of the required string.

G	H	I
Text	**Result**	**Formula text**
California - CA	California	=LEFT(G2,FIND("-",G2)-1)
Colorado - CO	Colorado	=LEFT(G3,FIND("-",G3)-1)
Connecticut - CT	Connecticut	=LEFT(G4,FIND("-",G4)-1)
Delaware - DE	DE	=RIGHT(G5,LEN(G5)-(FIND("-",G5)+1))
Florida - FL	FL	=RIGHT(G6,LEN(G6)-(FIND("-",G6)+1))
Georgia - GA	GA	=RIGHT(G7,LEN(G7)-(FIND("-",G7)+1))

=LEFT(G2,FIND("-",G2)-1)

FIND returns the position of "-", which is 12 in this case. We need to subtract 1 from this number to remove the divider from the part of the string we want to extract. The LEFT function then uses 10 as the starting point to return the characters in the string, starting from right to left. See the section **LEFT, RIGHT Functions** for more on the LEFT function.

LEFT and RIGHT Functions

The LEFT function returns the leftmost characters in a text string based on the number of characters you specify in one of its arguments. The RIGHT function returns the rightmost characters in a text string starting from the position you specify.

> **Tip** You can now use the new TEXTBEFORE and TEXTAFTER functions to extract text more easily than you could with the LEFT and RIGHT functions.

Syntax

=LEFT(text, [num_chars])

=RIGHT(text,[num_chars])

Arguments

Argument	Description
text	Required. This argument represents the text string with the characters you want to extract.
num_chars	Optional. An integer that specifies the number of characters you want to extract from the text. The count starts from the left for the LEFT function and the right for the RIGHT function.

Remarks

- If *num_chars* is larger than the length of *text*, the functions will return all characters in *text*.

- If *num_chars* is omitted, the functions return only the first character for the LEFT function and only the last character for the RIGHT function.

Example

In the example below, we use the LEFT and RIGHT functions to extract portions of text in different ways.

	A	B	C
1	Text	Result	Formula text
2	Alabama - AL	A	=LEFT(A2)
3	Alaska - AK	K	=RIGHT(A3)
4	Arizona - AZ	Arizona	=LEFT(A4,7)
5	Arkansas - AR	AR	=RIGHT(A5,2)
6	California - CA	California	=LEFT(A6,FIND("-",A6)-1)
7	Colorado - CO	Colorado	=LEFT(A7,FIND("-",A7)-1)
8	Connecticut - CT	Connecticut	=LEFT(A8,FIND("-",A8)-1)
9	Delaware - DE	DE	=RIGHT(A9,LEN(A9)-(FIND("-",A9)+1))
10	Florida - FL	FL	=RIGHT(A10,LEN(A10)-(FIND("-",A10)+1))
11	Georgia - GA	GA	=RIGHT(A11,LEN(A11)-(FIND("-",A11)+1))
12	Quanta Builders	Quanta	=LEFT(A12, FIND(" ",A12)-1)
13			
14			

Formula explanations

=LEFT(A2)

In the formula above, cell A2 is the text argument. There is no num_chars argument. Thus, LEFT returns the first character on the left of the string.

=RIGHT(A3)

This formula has cell A3 as the text argument, and there is no num_chars argument. Hence, RIGHT returns the last character in the string.

=LEFT(A4,7)

This formula has cell A4 as the text argument and 7 as the num_chars argument. It returns **Arizona**, 7 characters from the left of the string.

=RIGHT(A5,2)

This formula takes cell A4 as the text argument and 7 as the num_chars argument. It returns **AR**, 2 characters from the right of the string.

=LEFT(A6,FIND("-",A6)-1)

This formula takes cell A6 as the text argument. We calculate the num_chars argument using the FIND function to find and return the position of the hyphen character (-) in the text.

We then subtract 1 from the result to return the number of characters in the text before the hyphen. Hence **FIND("-",A6)-1** will return 10. The result is California. This formula will work for any piece of text separated by a hyphen where we want to extract the left portion.

=RIGHT(A9,LEN(A9)-(FIND("-",A9)+1))

This formula takes cell A9 as the text argument. We calculate the num_chars argument by using FIND to return the position of the hyphen character (-) in the text. We then add 1 to move to the position of the first character after the hyphen (on the right).

The LEN function is used to get the length of the string as we want to subtract the number of characters returned by FIND to give us the number of characters after the hyphen, which is 2 in this case.

This formula will work for a piece of text of any length separated by a hyphen, regardless of the position of the hyphen.

=LEFT(A12, FIND(" ",A12)-1)

This formula uses LEFT to return the string before the first space. A12 is the cell containing the string from which we want to extract text. **FIND(" ",A12)-1** returns the number of characters before the first space.

LEFTB, RIGHTB Functions

LEFTB and RIGHTB are variants of the LEFT and RIGHT functions that return characters in a text string based on the number of bytes you specify.

RIGHTB/LEFTB are for systems set to a default language that supports the double-byte character set (DBCS). The languages that support DBCS include Japanese, Traditional Chinese, Simplified Chinese, and Korean. If your system has a default language that supports DBCS, you would have LEFTB and RIGHTB in place of LEFT and RIGHT.

If your system has a default language that supports the single-byte character set (SBCS), LEFTB/RIGHTB will behave the same as LEFT/RIGHT, counting 1 byte per character.

MID Function

The MID function extracts a portion of a text from another text based on a specified starting position and the number of characters to be extracted.

> **Tip** For more complex text extractions, use the new TEXTBEFORE or TEXTAFTER functions. They're easier to use, offer more options, and can do most tasks you can do with MID.

Syntax

=MID(text, start_num, num_chars)

Arguments

Argument	Description
text	Required. A text string or a cell reference containing the characters you want to extract.
start_num	Required. A number that represents the starting point of the first character to extract from the value in *text*. The first character in *text* starts with 1. The second is 2, and so on.
num_chars	Required. A number specifying the number of characters you want to extract from *text*.

Remarks

- If the start_num argument is larger than the length of the string in the text argument, MID will return an empty text ("").

- MID will return the #VALUE! error if start_num is less than 1.

- MID returns the #VALUE! error if num_chars is a negative value.

Examples

The examples use the MID function to extract characters from several text values.

	A	B	C
1	**Text**	**Result**	**Formula text**
2	NWTCFV-91	NWTCFV	=MID(A2,1,LEN(A2)-3)
3	NWTCFV-90	90	=MID(A3,FIND("-",A3)+1,2)
4	NWT-100-CFV	100	=MID(A4,FIND("-",A4)+1,3)
5	01-345-4000	345	=MID(A5,4,3)
6	Andrew Steven James	Steven	=MID(A6,FIND(" ",A6)+1,FIND(" ",A6,FIND(" ",A6)+1)-FIND(" ",A6))
7	Minnesota(MN)	MN	=MID(A7,FIND("(",A7)+1,2)
8			
9			

Formula descriptions

=MID(A2,1,LEN(A2)-3)

Removes the last 3 characters in the text and returns the rest.

For this formula, A2 is the cell reference containing the string from which we want to extract text. We're starting from the first character, so start_num is 1. We want to return the length of the text except for the last 3 characters. We can use LEN to return this number for the num_chars argument.

=MID(A3,FIND("-",A3)+1,2)

Finds the hyphen in the text and returns the two characters after.

For this formula, A3 is the cell containing the string from which we want to extract text. We're starting from the first character after the hyphen "-", which we can identify with FIND("-",A3)+1. We want to return two characters, so 2 is the *num_chars* argument.

=MID(A5,4,3)

For this formula, A5 is the cell containing the string from which we want to extract characters. The first character to extract is 3, which starts at the fourth position, so we have 4 as our start_num. We want to return three characters, so we have 3 as the num_chars.

=MID(A6,FIND(" ",A6)+1,FIND(" ",A6,FIND(" ",A6)+1)-FIND(" ",A6))

This formula extracts the middle name from the full name.

The **text** argument is A6.

The **start_num** argument is FIND(" ",A6)+1. This nested formula identifies the position of the first character after the first space, which is 8.

The **num_chars** argument is FIND(" ",A6,FIND(" ",A6)+1)-FIND(" ",A6).

FIND(" ",A6,FIND(" ",A6)+1) finds the position of the second space, which is 14, and **FIND(" ",A6)** finds the position of the first space, which is 7.

We then subtract the position of the first space from the position of the second space like this **FIND(" ",A6,FIND(" ",A6)+1)-FIND(" ",A6)**, which is 14-7.

=MID(A7,FIND("(",A7)+1,2)

This formula finds the opening bracket in a string and returns the two characters after the bracket.

A7 is the cell containing the string from which we want to extract two characters. Our start_num is the position of the first character after the opening bracket "(", which we can identify with FIND("-",A3)+1. We want to return two characters, so 2 is the num_chars argument.

Split or Concatenate Text

The functions in this subcategory enable you to create formulas that can split a text into different columns or combine text from different columns into one cell.

TEXTSPLIT Function

The TEXTSPLIT function enables you to split text strings into different columns or rows. TEXTSPLIT is a dynamic array function that can take in one value and return multiple values. You can use the Text-to-Columns wizard in Excel for splitting text into columns, but TEXTSPLIT is easier to use and offers more splitting options.

 Note This function is currently only available in Excel for Microsoft 365.

Syntax

=TEXTSPLIT(text,col_delimiter,[row_delimiter],[ignore_empty], [match_mode], [pad_with])

Arguments

Argument	Description
text	Required. A value or cell reference representing the text you want to split.
col_delimiter	Required. The delimiter used to split the text into different columns.
row_delimiter	Optional. The delimiter used to split the text into different rows.
ignore_empty	Optional. Enter TRUE to ignore empty values, i.e., two or more consecutive delimiters without a value in-between them. Enter FALSE to create empty cells for empty values. FALSE is the default if this argument is omitted.

match_mode	Optional. Determines if case sensitivity is used to match the delimiter. Case sensitivity is used by default.
	0 = case-sensitive (default).
	1 = case-insensitive.
pad_with	Optional. A value to use for missing values in two-dimensional arrays. The default is #N/A.

Remarks:

If you set ignore_empty to TRUE, ensure there are no spaces between the consecutive delimiters. Otherwise, the feature to ignore empty values does not work.

Example 1 – Splitting into columns

The table below has examples of text being split into different columns using different delimiters.

Notice that you have to enter the delimiter precisely. For example, if there is a gap (or space) after a delimiter, you must enter that space after the delimiter in your formula to ensure blank spaces are not added to the split values. You can also use the TRIM function in your formula to remove any blank spaces from the result if the original text contains irregular spacing.

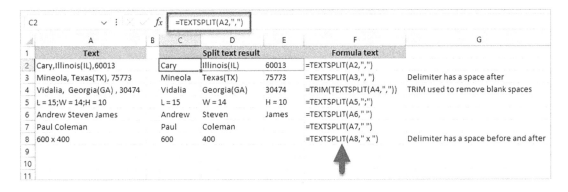

Example 2 – Splitting into rows

The example below splits the text in A13 into rows rather than columns. To split the text into rows, leave the col_delimiter argument empty, and enter the delimiter for the row_delimiter argument.

=TEXTSPLIT(A13,,", ")

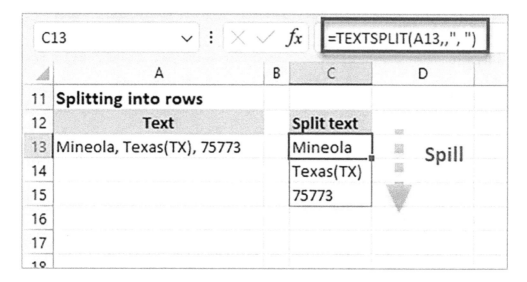

Example 3 – Splitting text with different delimiters

If the text values to be split have more than one delimiter type, you can use curly brackets to specify more than one delimiter for the col_delimiter argument. See the example below.

=TEXTSPLIT(A2,{",",";"})

C2			fx	=TEXTSPLIT(A2,{",",";"})			
	A	B	C	D	E	F	G
1	Text		Split text result				Formula text
2	NWTB-1,Chai,Beverages;18.00		NWTB-1	Chai	Beverages	18.00	=TEXTSPLIT(A2,{",",";"})
3							
4							
5							
6							

Example 4 – Two-dimensional splits

TEXTSPLIT allows you to split a text string into rows and columns simultaneously, where you specify delimiters for both the col_delimiter and row_delimiter arguments.

The example below splits the text in A2 into columns and rows by providing the following:

- The **col_delimiter** - an equal sign ("=")
- The **row_delimiter** - a semi-colon, and space "; "

The formula looks like this:

=TEXTSPLIT(A2,"=","; ")

The formula creates a 2D array made up of 2 columns and 3 rows:

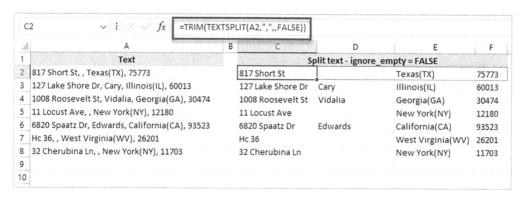

Example 5 – Handling empty values

In the example below, the text string to be split has empty values indicated by two or more consecutive delimiters. The formula below has been wrapped in TRIM to fix any inconsistent spacing.

By default, TEXTSPLIT will create empty cells for the missing values, as shown in the image below. You can also set the ignore_empty argument to FALSE to get the same result.

=TRIM(TEXTSPLIT(A2,","))

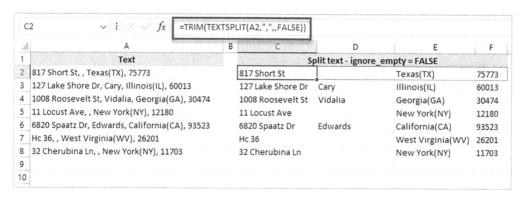

To ignore empty values, set the ignore_empty argument to TRUE, as shown in the formula below.

=TEXTSPLIT(A14,", ",,TRUE)

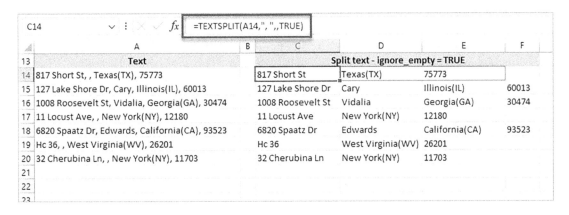

	A	B	C	D	E	F
13	**Text**		**Split text - ignore_empty = TRUE**			
14	817 Short St, , Texas(TX), 75773		817 Short St	Texas(TX)	75773	
15	127 Lake Shore Dr, Cary, Illinois(IL), 60013		127 Lake Shore Dr	Cary	Illinois(IL)	60013
16	1008 Roosevelt St, Vidalia, Georgia(GA), 30474		1008 Roosevelt St	Vidalia	Georgia(GA)	30474
17	11 Locust Ave, , New York(NY), 12180		11 Locust Ave	New York(NY)	12180	
18	6820 Spaatz Dr, Edwards, California(CA), 93523		6820 Spaatz Dr	Edwards	California(CA)	93523
19	Hc 36, , West Virginia(WV), 26201		Hc 36	West Virginia(WV)	26201	
20	32 Cherubina Ln, , New York(NY), 11703		32 Cherubina Ln	New York(NY)	11703	
21						
22						
23						

TEXTJOIN Function

TEXTJOIN is the opposite of TEXTSPLIT, as it enables you to combine text values from multiple cells into one string. The difference between TEXTJOIN and the CONCAT function is that TEXTJOIN has extra arguments that allow you to specify a delimiter as a separator. If your delimiter is a blank space, this function concatenates the ranges like CONCAT. This function also has options that allow you to ignore empty cells.

Syntax

=TEXTJOIN(delimiter, ignore_empty, text1, [text2], ...)

Arguments

Argument	Description
delimiter	Required. The character you want to use to separate text items in your string. The delimiter can be a string, one or more characters enclosed in double quotes, or a cell reference containing a text string. If this argument is a number, it will be treated as text.
ignore_empty	Required. Enter TRUE or FALSE. If the value is TRUE, Excel ignores empty cells.
text1	Required. The first text item to be joined. It can be a string, a cell reference, or a range with several cells.
[text2, ...]	Optional. Additional text items you want to join. You can have up to 252 arguments for the text items, including text1. Each can be a string, a cell reference, or a range with several cells.

Remarks

TEXTJOIN will return the #VALUE! error if the resulting string exceeds the cell limit of 32767 characters.

Example

In the following example, we use TEXTJOIN in C2:C7 to combine the First and Last name values from A2:A7 and B2:B7. The flexibility provided by TEXTJOIN enables us to swap the order of the names and separate them with a comma.

	A	B	C	D
1	**First name**	**Last name**	**Combined**	**Formula text**
2	Bruce	Henderson	Henderson, Bruce	=TEXTJOIN(", ", TRUE,B2,A2)
3	Louis	Anderson	Anderson, Louis	=TEXTJOIN(", ", TRUE,B3,A3)
4	Earl	Foster	Foster, Earl	=TEXTJOIN(", ", TRUE,B4,A4)
5	Sean	Hill	Hill, Sean	=TEXTJOIN(", ", TRUE,B5,A5)
6	Benjamin	Martinez	Martinez, Benjamin	=TEXTJOIN(", ", TRUE,B6,A6)
7	Joe	Perez	Perez, Joe	=TEXTJOIN(", ", TRUE,B7,A7)
8				
9	**Name**			
10	Bruce Henderson			
11	Louis Anderson			
12	Earl Foster			
13	Sean Hill			
14				
15	**Combined**			
16	Bruce Henderson, Louis Anderson, Earl Foster, Sean Hill			=TEXTJOIN(", ",TRUE,A10:A13)
17				

Explanation of formula

=TEXTJOIN(", ", TRUE,B2,A2)

The *delimiter* argument is a comma enclosed in quotes. The *ignore_empty* argument is TRUE because we want to ignore empty cells. The *text1* and *text2* arguments are cell references B2 and A2, representing the first and last names. The formula is copied to the other cells to populate the other results in the column.

> **Tip** You can now use the **Flash Fill** command on the Excel Ribbon to achieve the same results as above. It would be faster to use Flash Fill for this task in certain situations than a formula. If you want more information on Flash Fill, please see my book, *Excel 2022 Basics*.

=TEXTJOIN(", ",TRUE,A10:A13)

The second example uses the TEXTJOIN function to concatenate names in a range of cells (A10:A13) into a single string with a comma used as a separator.

CONCAT Function

The CONCAT function enables you to combine the text from multiple ranges or strings into one string. The function does not provide a delimiter, so you must add that manually in your formula. For example, =CONCAT("Hello"," ","world") will return *Hello world*. If you want to specify a delimiter, see the TEXTJOIN function.

> **Note** This function was introduced as a replacement for the CONCATENATE function. CONCATENATE is still available in Excel for backward compatibility, but it is recommended that you use CONCAT going forward.

Syntax

=CONCAT(text1, [text2],…)

Arguments

Argument	Description
text1	Required. This argument represents a text item to be joined. It could be a string or a range of cells with text.
[text2, …]	Optional. Additional text to be joined. You can have up to 253 arguments of text items to be joined. Each can be a string or a range of cells with text.

Remarks

- If the resulting string exceeds the cell limit of 32767 characters, CONCAT returns the #VALUE! error.

- You can use the TEXTJOIN function to include delimiters like spacing and/or commas between the texts you want to combine.

Example

In the example below, we used the CONCAT function differently to concatenate text from different cells.

	A	B	C	D	E
1	First name	Lastname		Result	Formula text
2	Bruce	Henderson		Bruce Henderson	=CONCAT(A2," ",B2)
3	Louis	Anderson		Bruce & Louis	=CONCAT(A2, " & ", A3)
4	Earl	Foster		Bruce and Louis did a good job.	=CONCAT(A2, " and ", A3, " did a good job.")
5				Anderson, Louis	=CONCAT(B3,", ",A3)
6				Anderson, Louis	=B3 & ", " & A3
7					
8					
9					

Explanation of formulas

=CONCAT(A2," ",B2)

This formula concatenates the text in A2 and B2 with an empty string in between, represented by the empty string in the formula.

=CONCAT(A2, " & ", A3)

This formula concatenates the text in cells A2 and A3 with an ampersand character (&) in the middle representing two first names.

=CONCAT(A2, " and ", A3, "did a good job.")

This formula uses the text in cells A2 and A3 to form part of a larger sentence.

=CONCAT(B3,", ",A3)

This formula concatenates the text in cells B3 and A3 with a comma in-between, representing the Last name and First name.

=B3 & ", " & A3

The formula above is for comparisons. It doesn't use CONCAT but achieves the same result using ampersands (Excel's concatenation operator).

Change the Case of Text Values

The functions in this category enable you to change the case of text values using formulas.

UPPER, LOWER, and PROPER Functions

The UPPER, LOWER, and PROPER functions are similar and take only one argument. UPPER converts all characters to uppercase, while LOWER converts all characters to lowercase. PROPER capitalizes the first character of every word in a string and converts all other characters to lowercase. A text string is a continuous stream of characters without spaces. Every letter after a space or punctuation character is capitalized.

Syntax

=UPPER(text)

=LOWER(text)

=PROPER(text)

Argument	Description
Text	Required. The text for which you want to change the case. This argument can be a cell reference or text string.

Example

In the example below, we use the UPPER, LOWER, and PROPER functions to change the case of the text values in column A. The results are in column B, and column C displays the formulas in column B.

	A	B	C
1	Text	Result	Formula text
2	NWTB-1	nwtb-1	=LOWER(A2)
3	NWTCO-3	nwtco-3	=LOWER(A3)
4	Beverages	BEVERAGES	=UPPER(A4)
5	Condiments	CONDIMENTS	=UPPER(A5)
6	Oil	OIL	=UPPER(A6)
7	Jams, Preserves	JAMS, PRESERVES	=UPPER(A7)
8	tesTinG capitalization now	Testing Capitalization Now	=PROPER(A8)
9	this is a TITLE	This Is A Title	=PROPER(A9)
10	bruce henderson	Bruce Henderson	=PROPER(A10)
11	louis anderson	Louis Anderson	=PROPER(A11)
12	Earl foster	Earl Foster	=PROPER(A12)
13	sean hiLL	Sean Hill	=PROPER(A13)
14	benjamiN MartineZ	Benjamin Martinez	=PROPER(A14)
15			

Chapter 8

Financial Functions

This chapter covers functions used to calculate the following:

- Present value of an investment or a loan.

- Future value of an investment.

- Net present value of an investment taking cash flows into account.

- Monthly payments for a loan over a given period.

- Straight-line depreciation of an asset over a period.

- Sum-of-years' digits depreciation of an asset over a period.

- Fixed-declining balance depreciation of an asset over a given period.

- Double-declining balance depreciation of an asset over a given period.

Y ou can access financial functions in Excel by clicking the Financial button, in the Function Library group, on the Formulas tab. Most of the financial functions in Excel are specialized functions used for financial accounting.

Definitions

Most of the financial functions in Excel have arguments that are acronyms for financial terms. For example, terms like PV (Present Value), FV (Future Value), PMT (Payment), and IPMT (interest payment) show up as arguments in many functions. It is important to understand the terminology to better understand these functions. The following section covers some key terms used.

Annuity

An annuity is a series of regular cash payments over a certain period. For example, a mortgage or a car loan is an annuity. An investment that pays regular dividends is also an annuity. Most of the functions covered in this chapter are known as annuity functions.

PV (Present Value)

PV is the present value of an investment based on a constant growth rate. It is the lump-sum amount that a series of future payments is worth right now.

FV (Future Value)

FV is the future value of an investment based on a constant rate of growth. Imagine a scenario where you need to save $25,000 to pay for a project in 20 years. In that case, $25,000 is the future value. To calculate how much you need to save monthly, you'll also need to factor in an assumed interest rate over the period.

PMT (Payment)

PMT is the payment made for each period in the annuity. Usually, the payment includes the principal plus interest (without any other fees) set over the life of the annuity. For example, a $100,000 mortgage over 25 years at 3% interest would have monthly payments of $474. You would enter -474 into the formula as the *pmt*.

RATE

RATE is the interest rate per period. For example, a loan at a 6% annual interest rate will have an interest rate of 6%/12 per month.

NPER (Number of periods)

NPER is the number of payment periods for a loan or investment based on constant periodic payments and a constant interest rate. For example, a three-year loan with monthly payments will have 36 periods (3 x 12). Hence, the *nper* argument would be 3*12 for such a scenario.

> **Note** The FV, PV, and PMT arguments can be positive or negative, depending on whether you are paying or receiving money. The values will be negative if you're paying out money and positive if you're receiving money.

Calculating Investments and Loans

The functions in this category enable you to build formulas that calculate annuities like the value of investments and loans.

PV Function

The PV function calculates the present value of an investment (or a loan), assuming a constant interest rate. The present value is the amount a series of future payments is currently worth. You can use PV with regular payments (such as a mortgage or other loan), periodic payments, or the future value of a lump sum paid now.

Syntax

=PV(rate, nper, pmt, [fv], [type])

Arguments

See the Definitions section above for a more detailed description of these arguments.

Arguments	Description
rate	Required. The interest rate per period.
nper	Required. The total number of payment periods in an annuity.
pmt	Required. The payment made for each period in the annuity.
	If you omit *pmt*, you must include the *fv* argument.
fv	Optional. This argument is the future value of an investment based on an assumed rate of growth.
	If you omit fv, it is assumed to be 0 (zero). For example, the future value of a loan is 0. If you omit fv, then you must include the pmt argument.
type	Optional. This argument is 0 or 1 and indicates when payments are due.
	0 or omitted = at the end of the period.
	1 = at the beginning of the period.

Remarks

- You must always specify the rate argument in the same units as the nper argument. For example, say you have monthly payments on a three-year loan at 5% annual interest. If you use 5%/12 for *rate*, you must use 3*12 for *nper*. If the payments on the same loan are being made annually, then you would use 5% for rate and 3 for nper.

- In annuity functions, the cash paid out (like a payment to savings) is represented by a negative number. The cash received (like a dividend payment) is represented by a positive number. For example, a $500 deposit would be represented by -500 for the depositor and by 500 for the bank.

Example

In the example below, we use the PV formula to calculate:

1. The present value of a $500 monthly payment over 25 years at a rate of 1.5% interest.

2. The present value of the lump sum that is needed now to create $20,000 in 10 years at a rate of 3.5% interest.

E4				*fx*	=PV(A4/12,B4*12,C4)	
	A	B	C	D	E	F
1	**Present Value (PV)**					
2						
3	**Annual Interest Rate**	**Term (years)**	**Payment**	**Future Value**	**Present Value**	**Formula text**
4	1.50%	25	($500.00)		$125,019.90	=PV(A4/12,B4*12,C4)
5	3.50%	10		$20,000.00	($14,100.94)	=PV(A5/12,B5*12,,D5)
6						
7						
8						
9						
10						
11						

Explanation of Formulas:

=PV(A4/12,B4*12,C4)

As you've probably noticed, the units for *rate* and *nper* have been kept consistent by specifying them in monthly terms, A4/12 and B4*12. The payment (pmt) has been entered in the worksheet as a negative value as this is money being paid out.

=PV(A5/12,B5*12,,D5)

The present value is a negative number as it shows the amount of cash that needs to be invested today (paid out) to generate the future value of $20,000 in 10 years at a rate of 3.5% interest.

FV Function

The FV function calculates an investment's future value (at a specified date in the future) based on a constant interest rate. You can use FV to calculate the future value of regular, periodic, or a single lump-sum payment.

Syntax

=FV(rate,nper,pmt,[pv],[type])

Arguments

Arguments	Description
rate	Required. The interest rate per period.
nper	Required. The total number of payment periods.
pmt	Required. The payment made for each period in the annuity.
	If you omit pmt, you must include pv.
pv	Optional. The present value of an investment based on a constant growth rate.
	If you omit pv, it is assumed to be 0 (zero), and you must include pmt.
type	Optional. The *type* is 0 or 1, indicating when payments are due.
	0 (or omitted) = at the end of the period.
	1 = at the beginning of the period.

Remarks

- You must always specify the rate argument in the same units as the nper argument. For example, say you have monthly payments on a three-year loan at 5% annual interest. If you use 5%/12 for *rate*, you must use 3*12 for *nper*. If the payments on the same loan are being made annually, then you would use 5% for rate and 3 for nper.

- In annuity functions, the cash paid out (like a payment to savings) is represented by a negative number. The cash received (like a dividend payment) is represented by a positive number. For example, a $500 deposit would be represented by -500 for the depositor and by 500 for the bank.

Example

The example below uses the FV function to calculate:

1. The future value of a monthly payment of $200 over 10 months at an interest of 6% per annum.

2. The future value of a lump sum of $1,000 plus 12 monthly payments of $100 at an interest rate of 6%.

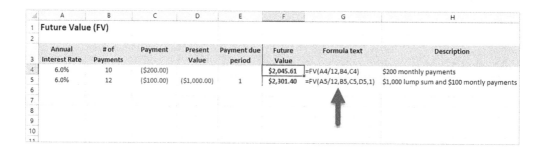

	A	B	C	D	E	F	G	H
1	Future Value (FV)							
2								
3	Annual Interest Rate	# of Payments	Payment	Present Value	Payment due period	Future Value	Formula text	Description
4	6.0%	10	($200.00)			$2,045.61	=FV(A4/12,B4,C4)	$200 monthly payments
5	6.0%	12	($100.00)	($1,000.00)	1	$2,301.40	=FV(A5/12,B5,C5,D5,1)	$1,000 lump sum and $100 montly payments
6								
7								
8								
9								
10								

Explanation of Formulas:

=FV(A4/12,B4,C4)

Note that the *rate* argument has been divided by 12 to represent monthly payments. The *pmt* argument is a negative value (C4) as this is money being paid out.

=FV(A5/12,B5,C5,D5,1)

This formula has the pmt argument and the optional pv argument, which represents the present value of the investment. The payment due period is 1, which means the payment starts at the beginning of the period.

NPV Function

The NPV function calculates the net present value, which is the present value of cash inflows and cash outflows over a period. It calculates the present value of an investment by applying a discount rate and a series of future payments that may be income (positive values) or payments/losses (negative values).

Syntax

=NPV(rate,value1,[value2],...)

Arguments

Argument	Description
Rate	Required. This argument is the percentage rate of discount over the length of the investment.
Value1	Required. This argument represents either a payment/loss (negative value) or income (positive value).
value2, ...	Optional. You can have additional values representing payments and income up to 254 value arguments.
	The length of time between these payments must be equally spaced and occur at the end of each period.

Remarks

- The rate argument in the function might represent the rate of inflation or the interest rate you might get from an alternative form of investment, such as a high-yield savings account.

- The value arguments represent the projected income (or loss) values over the period of the investment.

- Ensure you enter the payment and income values in the correct order because NPV uses the order of the value arguments to interpret the order of cash flows.

- The NPV investment begins one period before the date of the first cash flow (value1) and ends with the last cash flow (valueN) in the list of value arguments. If the first cash flow happens at the beginning of the period, you must add it to the result of the NPV function and not include it as one of its value arguments.

- The main difference between NPV and PV is that with PV, the cash flows can start at the beginning or end of the period, while for NPV, the cash flows start at the beginning of the period. Also, PV has the same cash flow amount throughout the investment, while NPV can have different cash flow amounts.

- Arguments that are not numbers are ignored.

Example

The example below calculates the net present value of an initial investment of $50,000 over five years, considering an annual discount rate of 2.5 percent.

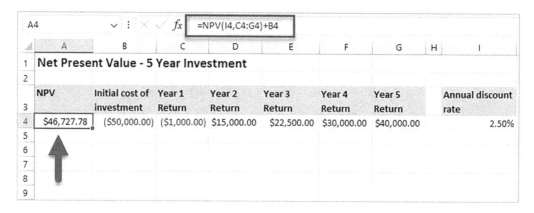

Formula explanation

=NPV(I4,C4:G4)+B4

In the figure above, Year 1 of the investment shows a loss of $1,000. Hence, Year 1 has been entered as a negative value. The other years of the investment (years two to five) returned profits, which were entered as positive values.

The function uses two arguments, the *rate* and *value1*, which references cells C4:G4. The initial investment is added to the result returned by the function rather than being an argument in the function.

The result shows the investment's net present value over five years is $46,727.78.

PMT Function

The PMT function calculates the payment of a loan on regular payments and a constant interest rate over a period. The PMT function is often used to calculate the repayment of a mortgage with a fixed interest rate.

Syntax

=PMT(rate, nper, pv, [fv], [type])

Arguments

Arguments	Description
rate	Required. The interest rate per period.
nper	Required. The total number of payment periods.
pv	Required. This argument is the present value of a principal or a series of future payments.
fv	Optional. This argument is the future value of an investment based on an assumed growth rate.
	If you omit fv, it is assumed to be 0 (zero), i.e., the future value of a loan is 0.
type	Optional. This argument is 0 or 1 and indicates when payments are due.
	0 (or omitted) = at the end of the period.
	1 = at the beginning of the period.

Remarks

- The payment returned by PMT is for the principal and interest. It does not include taxes, reserve payments, or other loan fees.

- You must always specify the *rate* argument in the same units as the *nper* argument. For example, say you have monthly payments on a three-year loan at 5% annual interest. If you use 5%/12 for *rate*, you must use 3*12 for *nper*. If the payments on the same loan are being made annually, then you would use 5% for rate and 3 for nper.

> **-Tip** To calculate the total amount paid over the duration of the loan, simply multiply the value returned by PMT by the number of payments (nper).

Example

In the example below, we calculate the PMT for two loans:

- A $10,000 loan over 12 payments at 8.0 percent interest.
- A $10,000 loan over 60 payments at 4.9 percent interest.

	A	B	C	D	E
1	**Payment (PMT)**				
2					
3	**Annual Interest Rate**	**# of payments**	**Loan amount**	**PMT**	**Formula text**
4	8.0%	12	$10,000.00	($869.88)	=PMT(A4/12,B4,C4)
5	4.9%	60	$10,000.00	($188.25)	=PMT(A5/12,B5,C5)
6					
7					
8					
9					
10					

Formula explanation

=PMT(A4/12,B4,C4)

The rate argument is the value in cell A4 divided by 12 to represent the interest rate in monthly terms because nper (in cell B4) is also specified in monthly terms. The pv argument is C4, which is the present value of the loan, $10,000.

Result: A monthly payment of $869.88 pays the loan off in 12 months.

=PMT(A5/12,B5,C5)

This formula is also for a loan of $10,000. However, the nper is 60, and the rate is 4.9 percent.

Result: A monthly payment of $188.25 pays the loan off in 60 months (5 years).

Calculating Depreciation

The functions in this section enable you to create formulas that calculate the depreciation of an asset using various depreciation methods.

SLN Function

The SLN function is a depreciation function and calculates the straight-line depreciation of an asset over a period. It depreciates the asset by the same amount each year.

Syntax

=SLN(cost, salvage, life)

Arguments

Argument	Description
cost	Required. The initial cost of the depreciating asset.
salvage	Required. The value at the end of the depreciation (also referred to as the salvage value of the asset).
life	Required. The number of periods over which the asset is depreciating (also known as the useful life of the asset).

Example

In the example below, we have a report calculating the SLN depreciation of a couple of cars with a useful life of 10 years.

| E4 | | | | fx | =SLN(B4,D4,C4) | |

▲	A	B	C	D	E	F
1	Company car - straight-line depreciation (SLN)					
2						
3	Car	Cost	Yrs of useful life	Salvage value	Yearly depreciation allowance	Formula text
4	Car 1	$20,000.00	10	$2,500.00	$1,750.00	=SLN(B4,D4,C4)
5	Car 2	$30,000.00	10	$7,500.00	$2,250.00	=SLN(B5,D5,C5)
6	Car 3	$45,000.00	10	$10,000.00	$3,500.00	=SLN(B6,D6,C6)
7						
8						
9						
10						
11						

Formula explanation

=SLN(B4,D4,C4)

In the formula above for **Car 1**, the cost references cell B4 ($20,000). The salvage value references cell D4 ($2,500). The life is C4 (10 years).

The formula returns $1,750, which is the yearly depreciation allowance to be made for the car. When listing this asset on the company's balance sheet, this value would be subtracted from the car's value.

The formula in E4 was copied down using the cell's fill handle to calculate the SLN value of the other cars on the list.

SYD Function

The SYD function (sum of years' digits) is a depreciation function that returns an asset's sum-of-years' digits depreciation over a specified period.

Syntax

=SYD(cost, salvage, life, per)

Arguments

Argument	Description
cost	Required. The initial cost of the asset you're depreciating.
salvage	Required. The value at the end of the depreciation (also referred to as the salvage value of the asset).
life	Required. The number of periods over which the asset is depreciated (also referred to as the useful life of the asset).
per	Required. The period for which to calculate the depreciation. It must be in the same units as life. For example, the period for the third year of an asset with a ten-year life will be 3.

Example

In the example below, we use the SYD function to calculate the depreciation of some office equipment over 10 years.

Function arguments:

- Cost = $40,000
- Life = 10 (years)
- Salvage = $1,000

B9				fx	=SYD(InitialCost,SalvageValue,Life,A9)	

⊿	A	B	C	D	E	F
1	Depreciation of office equipment - SYD					
2						
3	Initial Cost	$40,000.00		InitialCost = B3		
4	Life (years)	10		Life = B4		
5	Salvage value	$1,000.00		SalvageValue = B5		
6						
7	Year	SYD	Asset value			
8	0	$0.00	$40,000.00			
9	1	$7,090.91	$32,909.09			
10	2	$6,381.82	$26,527.27			
11	3	$5,672.73	$20,854.55			
12	4	$4,963.64	$15,890.91			
13	5	$4,254.55	$11,636.36		Cumulative	
14	6	$3,545.45	$8,090.91		depreciation	
15	7	$2,836.36	$5,254.55			
16	8	$2,127.27	$3,127.27			
17	9	$1,418.18	$1,709.09			
18	10	$709.09	$1,000.00			
19						

Formula explanation

=SYD(InitialCost,SalvageValue,Life,A9)

The formula in cell B9 uses the following range names for the cost, salvage, and life arguments:

- InitialCost = B3

- Life = B4

- SalvageValue = B5

The values in the cells above remain the same over the 10-year depreciation period, so using range names makes it easier to copy the formula for the other years. The *per* argument is a relative reference, cell A9, which changes with the year being calculated.

As depicted in the image above, with the SYD function, the depreciation amount gets progressively smaller compared to an SLN depreciation, for example, which is constant over the period.

=C8-SYD(InitialCost,SalvageValue,Life,A9)

The formulas in the **Asset value** column (C9:C18) subtract each year's depreciation from the previous year's calculated asset value. Hence, this column shows a progressive decrease in the asset's value over the 10-year period until it reaches the salvage value.

DB Function

The DB function is a depreciation function that uses the fixed-declining balance method to return the depreciation of an asset over a specified period. The fixed-declining balance method calculates the depreciation at a fixed rate.

Syntax

=DB(cost, salvage, life, period, [month])

Arguments

Arguments	Descriptions
cost	Required. The initial cost of the depreciating asset.
salvage	Required. The value at the end of the depreciation (also referred to as the salvage value of the asset).
life	Required. The number of periods over which the asset is depreciating (also referred to as the useful life of the asset).
period	Required. The period in the asset's life for which to calculate the depreciation. The period must be in the same units as life.
month	Optional. The number of months in the first year of the depreciation if it is not 12. If this argument is omitted, the default is 12.

Remarks

- The following formulas are used to calculate depreciation for a period:

  (cost - total depreciation from prior periods) * rate

  Where:

  rate = 1 - ((salvage / cost) ^ (1 / life))

- DB uses different formulas to calculate the depreciation for the first and last periods.

  First period:

cost * rate * month / 12

Last period:

((cost - total depreciation from prior periods) * rate * (12 - month)) / 12

Example 1

In the following example, we're calculating the depreciation of an asset over 5 years using the following data:

Argument	Value
Costs	$10,000
Salvage value	$2,000
Life	5 years

The first year has 12 months, so we can omit the month argument.

The formula for the **first year** will be thus:

=DB(10000, 2000, 5, 1)

Result: $2,750.00

Example 2

The following example calculates the depreciation of an asset with the following parameters:

Parameter	Value
Costs	$10,000
Salvage value	$2,000
Life (years)	5
Period (year)	5th year

First year (months)   8

The depreciation is calculated for the fifth year, and there are 8 months in the first year:

=DB(10000, 2000, 5, 5, 8)

Result: $855.84

Example 3

In this example, we use the SYD function to calculate the depreciation of office equipment with a useful life of 10 years. The initial cost is $40,000, and the salvage value is $1,000.

The first year has only 7 months, so we need to specify that in the *month* argument.

| B9 | | ✓ ⋮ ✕ ✓ *fx* | =DB(InitialCost,Salvage,Life,A9,FirstYr) | |

▲	A	B	C	D	E
1	**Depreciation of office equipment - (DB)**				
2					
3	Initial Cost	$40,000.00		*InitialCost = B3*	
4	Life (years)	10		*Life = B4*	
5	Salvage value	$1,000.00		*Salvage = B5*	
6	First Yr (# of months)	7		*FirstYr = B6*	
7					
8	**Year**	**DB**	**Asset value**		
9	1	$7,186.67	$32,813.33		
10	2	$10,106.51	$22,706.83		
11	3	$6,993.70	$15,713.12		
12	4	$4,839.64	$10,873.48		
13	5	$3,349.03	$7,524.45		
14	6	$2,317.53	$5,206.92		
15	7	$1,603.73	$3,603.19		
16	8	$1,109.78	$2,493.41		
17	9	$767.97	$1,725.44		
18	10	$531.43	$1,194.00		
19					

Formula explanation

=DB(InitialCost,Salvage,Life,A9,FirstYr)

The formula in cell B9 uses the following range names:
- InitialCost = B3
- Salvage = B4
- Life = B5
- FirstYr = B6

The range names correspond to the *cost*, *salvage*, *life*, and *month* arguments, as these remain the same over the 10-year depreciation period. The *per* argument is a relative reference, which changes in column A according to the year being calculated.

The *month* argument, FirstYr, holds a value of 7. This value specifies that the first year of the depreciation is 7 months rather than 12. This argument could have been omitted if the first year was 12 months.

From the image above, we can see that apart from the first year (7 months), the depreciation progresses linearly as the asset value reduces.

DDB Function

This DDB function returns the depreciation of an asset for a specified period using the double-declining balance method. The double-declining balance method calculates depreciation at an accelerated rate, with the depreciation highest in the first period and decreasing in successive periods.

This function is flexible, as you can change the *factor* argument if you don't want to use the double-declining balance method.

Syntax

=DDB(cost, salvage, life, period, [factor])

Arguments

Argument	Description
cost	Required. The initial cost of the depreciating asset.
salvage	Required. The value at the end of the depreciation (also referred to as the salvage value of the asset).
life	Required. The number of periods over which the asset is depreciating (also referred to as the useful life of the asset).
period	Required. The period in the asset's life for which to calculate the depreciation. It must be in the same units as life.
factor	Optional. The rate at which the balance declines.
	If omitted, the factor is assumed to be 2, which is the double-declining balance method.

Remarks

- The five arguments must be positive numbers.

- The DDB function uses the following formula to calculate depreciation for a period:

```
Min( (cost - total depreciation from prior periods) *
(factor/life), (cost - salvage - total depreciation from
prior periods) )
```

Example

In the following example, we use different DDB formulas to return results for the depreciation of a car.

Data:
- Initial Cost: $25,000.00
- Salvage value: $2,500.00
- Life (in years): 10

⁄⁄	A	B	C	D
1	**Depreciation of car - DDB**			
2				
3	Initial Cost	$25,000.00		
4	Salvage value	$2,500.00		
5	Life (in years)	10		
6				
7	**Period**	**Depreciation**	**Formula text**	
8	First day	$13.70	=DDB(Cost,Salvage,LifeInYrs*365,1)	*Factor 2 (default)*
9	First month	$416.67	=DDB(Cost,Salvage,LifeInYrs*12,1)	
10	First year	$5,000.00	=DDB(Cost,Salvage,LifeInYrs,1)	
11	First year (factor of 1.5)	$3,750.00	=DDB(Cost,Salvage,LifeInYrs,1,1.5)	*For comparisons*
12	Tenth year	$671.09	=DDB(Cost,Salvage,LifeInYrs,10)	
13				
14	*Cost = B3*			
15	*Salvage = B4*			
16	*LifeInYrs = B5*			
17				

Explanation of formulas

=DDB(Cost,Salvage,LifeInYrs*365,1)

The above formula uses range names for cell references:
- Cost = B3
- Salvage = B4
- LifeInYrs = B5

These range names relate to the *cost*, *salvage*, and *life* arguments in the formula.

Life is (10 * 365) because we want to calculate the depreciation in daily units rather than months or years. The period is 1, representing the first day of the item's life. The factor argument is omitted, so it defaults to 2, using the double-declining balance method.

=DDB(Cost,Salvage,LifeInYrs*12,1,2)

The formula above calculates the first month's depreciation. The factor argument was included in this case to specify the double-declining balance method. However, omitting the factor defaults to 2.

=DDB(Cost,Salvage,LifeInYrs,1)

The first year's depreciation. Notice that the *life* argument LifeInYrs has not been multiplied by 12, so the formula will return a result for year 1 as specified in the period argument.

=DDB(Cost,Salvage,LifeInYrs,1,1.5)

This formula is the first year's depreciation using a factor of 1.5 instead of the double-declining balance method.

=DDB(Cost,Salvage,LifeInYrs,10)

The above formula returns the tenth year's depreciation calculation. Factor has been omitted, so it defaults to 2.

Getting More Help with Functions

In deciding which functions to cover from each category, relevancy to the average user has been considered. Some Excel functions require specialist knowledge in certain professional areas, for example, Engineering, to be relevant, so they have not been covered here.

To get more help with these specialist functions, press F1 in the Excel window to display the Help panel. Then type "Excel functions" in the search bar. This gives you a list of Excel functions grouped by category or alphabetical order.

When you identify the function you want, you can visit its details page for a detailed description of the function and its arguments.

You can also visit Microsoft's online help for Excel functions which has the same information as the internal help in Excel.

Web link:
https://support.office.com/en-us/article/excel-functions-alphabetical-b3944572-255d-4efb-bb96-c6d90033e188

You can also visit our website for Excel tips:
https://www.excelbytes.com

Appendix

Keyboard Shortcuts for Functions and Formulas

T he table below covers some of the most useful Excel for Windows shortcut keys when working with functions, formulas, and the formula bar.

Keystroke	Action
F2	Moves the insertion point to the end of the contents of the active cell.
Ctrl+Shift+U	Expands or reduces the size of the formula bar.
Esc	Cancels an entry in the formula bar or a cell.
Enter	Confirms an entry in the formula bar and moves to the cell below.
Ctrl+End	Moves the cursor to the end of the contents in the formula bar.

Ctrl+Shift+End	Selects everything in the formula bar from the current position of the cursor to the end.
F9	Calculates all worksheets in all open workbooks.
Shift+F9	Calculates the active worksheet.
Ctrl+Alt+F9	Calculates all worksheets in all open workbooks, even if they have not changed since the last calculation.
Ctrl+Alt+Shift+F9	Checks all dependent formulas and then calculates all cells in all open workbooks.
Ctrl+A	Opens the Function Arguments dialog box when the insertion point is to the right of a function name in a formula bar.
Ctrl+Shift+A	Inserts the argument names and parentheses for a function when the insertion point is to the right of a function name in the formula bar.
Ctrl+E	Executes the Flash Fill command to fill down the current column if Excel recognizes patterns in the values in adjacent columns.
F4	Changes the selected cell reference or range in the formula bar to absolute references. Further presses will cycle through all combinations of absolute and relative references for the selected cell reference or range.
Shift+F3	Opens the Insert Function dialog box.
Ctrl+Shift+Quotation mark (")	Copies the value from the cell directly above the active cell into the active cell or formula bar.
Alt+F1	Automatically inserts an embedded chart of the data in the selected range.
F11	Automatically inserts a chart of the data in the selected range in a different worksheet.
Alt+M, M, D	Opens the New Name dialog box for creating a named range.
F3	Opens the Paste Name dialog box if a range name has been defined in the workbook.
Alt+F8	Opens the Macro dialog box where you can run, edit, or delete a macro.
Alt+F11	Opens the Visual Basic for Applications editor.

Glossary

Absolute reference

An absolute reference is a cell reference that doesn't change when you copy a formula containing the reference to another cell. For example, $A$3 means the row and column have been set to absolute.

Active cell

The cell that is currently selected and open for editing.

Alignment

The way a cell's contents are arranged within that cell, which could be left, centered, or right.

Array

An array can be seen as a row of values, a column of values, or a combination of both.

Argument

The input values a function requires to carry out a calculation.

AutoCalculate

AutoCalculate is an Excel feature that automatically calculates and displays the summary of a selected range of figures on the status bar.

AutoComplete

AutoComplete is an Excel feature that completes data entry for a range of cells based on values in other cells in the same column or row.

Backstage view

The Backstage view is the screen you see when you click the File tab on the Ribbon. It has several menu options for managing your workbook and configuring global settings in Excel.

Boolean array

A Boolean array is an array of TRUE/FALSE Boolean values or (0 and 1). In Excel, you can create such an array by applying logical tests to the values in a column or row.

Cell reference

The letter and number combination representing the intersection of a column and row. For example, B10 means column B, row 10.

Conditional format

A conditional format is a cell format applied when the cell content meets certain criteria.

Conditional formula

A conditional formula calculates a value from one of two expressions based on whether a third expression evaluates to true or false.

Dynamic array formula

Dynamic array formulas are a set of new formulas in Excel that enable you to return multiple results to a range of cells from one formula. This is called the spill range.

Excel table

An Excel table is a range defined as a table in Excel. Excel adds certain attributes to the range to make it easier to manipulate the data as a table.

Fill handle

This feature is the plus sign (+) at the lower-right of the selected cell that can be dragged to AutoFill values of other cells.

Fill Series

An Excel feature that allows you to create a series of values based on a starting value, including any rules or intervals.

Formula

An expression used to calculate a value.

Formula bar

The formula bar is the area just above the worksheet grid that displays the value of the active cell. You can enter your formula directly in the formula bar.

Function

A function is a predefined Excel formula that requires input values (arguments) to calculate and return a value.

Named range

A group of cells in your worksheet is given one name that can be used as a reference.

PivotTable

A PivotTable is an Excel summary table that allows you to dynamically summarize data from different perspectives. PivotTables are highly flexible, and you can quickly adjust them depending on how you need to display your results.

Quick Access Toolbar

A customizable toolbar with a set of commands independent of the current Excel tab being displayed.

Relative reference

Excel cell references are relative references by default. When formulas are copied to other cells, the cell references change based on the relative position of rows and columns.

Ribbon

The top part of the Excel window containing the tabs and commands.

Range

A group of cells in an Excel worksheet. For example, A1:B10 is a range.

Sort

A sort means to reorder the data in a worksheet based on a criterion. So, you could sort in ascending order or in descending order.

Spill Range

This is the range of cells that contains the results returned from an array formula. A spill range can be multiple rows and/or columns.

Workbook

A workbook is an Excel document that can contain one or more worksheets.

Worksheet

A worksheet is like a page in an Excel workbook.

Index

About The Author

Nathan George is a computer science graduate with several years of experience in the IT services industry in different roles, which included Excel VBA programming, Access development, Excel training, and providing end-user support to Excel power users. One of his main interests is using computers to automate tasks and increase productivity. As an author, he has written several technical and non-technical books.

Your feedback is important. If you found this book helpful, I would be very grateful if you can spend just 5 minutes leaving a customer review. You can go to the link below to leave a customer review.

https://www.excelbytes.com/functions-review

Thank you very much!

Other Books by Author

Excel 2022 Basics

A Quick and Easy Guide to Boosting Your Productivity with Excel

A Step-By-Step Approach to Learning Excel Fast!

Excel 2022 Basics covers all you need to get up to speed in creating Excel solutions for your data. This book covers all the features, commands, and functions you'll need for everyday Excel use in your job, business, or home.

Excel 2022 Basics comes with practical examples relevant to real-world Excel productivity tasks. To enable you to learn faster, this book comes with free downloadable practice files for all examples in the book using a sizable amount of sample data.

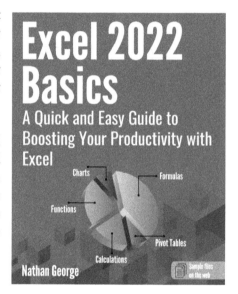

For more details, go to:

https://www.excelbytes.com/excel-books

296

Excel 2019 Macros and VBA

An Introduction to Excel Programming

Take your Excel skills to the next level with macros and Visual Basic for Applications (VBA)!

Create solutions that would have otherwise been too cumbersome or impossible to create with standard Excel commands and functions. Automate Excel for repetitive tasks and save yourself time and tedium.

With *Excel 2019 Macros and VBA*, you'll learn how to automate Excel using quick macros as well as writing VBA code. You'll learn all the VBA fundamentals to enable you to start creating your own code from scratch.

For more details, go to:

https://www.excelbytes.com/excel-books

Mastering Access 365

An Easy Guide to Building Efficient Databases for Managing Your Data

Has your data become too large and complex for Excel? If so, then Access may be the tool you need. Whether you're new to Access or looking to refresh your skills on this popular database application, you'll find everything you need to create efficient and robust database solutions for your data in this book.

Mastering Access 365 offers straightforward step-by-step explanations with practical examples for hands-on learning. This book covers Access for Microsoft 365 and Access 2021.

Available at Amazon:

https://www.excelbytes.com/access-book

www.ingramcontent.com/pod-product-compliance
Lightning Source LLC
LaVergne TN
LVHW082035050326
832904LV00005B/183